THE PERFORMANCE OF SELF
IN STUDENT WRITING

THE PERFORMANCE OF SELF IN STUDENT WRITING

THOMAS NEWKIRK

Boynton/Cook Publishers
HEINEMANN
Portsmouth, NH

Heinemann
A division of Reed Elsevier Inc.
361 Hanover Street
Portsmouth, NH 03801–3912

Offices and agents throughout the world

Library of Congress Cataloging-in-Publication Data
Newkirk, Thomas.
 The performance of self in student writing / Thomas Newkirk.
  p. cm.
 Includes bibliographical references and index.
 ISBN 0-86709-439-7 (acid-free paper)
 1. English language—Rhetoric—Study and teaching. 2. English
language—Rhetoric—Psychological aspects. 3. Report writing—
Psychological aspects. 4. Self-actualization (Psychology)
5. College students—Psychology. 6. Autobiography—Authorship.
7. Identity (Psychology) I. Title.
PE1404.N53 1997
808'.042'07—dc21   97-38280
                                                                                          CIP

Editors: Toby Gordon and Scott Mahler
Production: Vicki Kasabian
Cover design: Barbara Werden
Manufacturing: Louise Richardson

Printed in the United States of America on acid-free paper
01 00   DA   2 3 4 5

*It is probably no mere historical accident
that the word* person, *in its first meaning, is a mask.
It is rather a recognition of the fact that everybody is always
and everywhere, more or less consciously, playing a role. . . .
In a sense, and in so far as this mask represents the
conception we have formed of ourselves—the role we are
striving to live up to—this mask is our truer self, the self we
would like to be. In the end our conception of our role
becomes second nature and an integral part of our
personality. We come into the world as individuals,
achieve character, and become persons.*

— ROBERT EZRA PARK —

Contents

Acknowledgments

This book arose from conversations with graduate students and colleagues. I believe all of us shared a sense that there was something missing in the debate about postmodernism and personal writing. There was also a tone of dismissal that we resented. Yet at the same time scholars like James Berlin, John Trimbur, and Susan Miller, among others, were raising interesting questions that needed to be addressed. I want to thank a group of stimulating graduate students—Lance Svehla, Carol Kountz, Tim Dansdill, Michelle Payne, Mary Hallet, Don Jones, and the entire pragmatism course group. Additional thanks to Mary for reading a draft of the book.

Special thanks to Xiao-ming Li whose work on U. S. and Chinese traditions of reading student writing was especially useful. Also to Lad Tobin who, over breakfast at the Bagelry and climbs up Mt. Chocorua, listened to much of this. He, too, was a helpful reader of the manuscript. His own work into the nature of reading continues to instruct me in my work.

I have benefited from the work of other faculty in the English department at the University of New Hampshire. Pat Sullivan, particularly in her brilliant talk at UNH's 1994 writing conference, has shown how productive the cultural studies frame is for looking at student writing. Sarah Sherman gave me a crash course in the reevaluation of sentimentalism in American literature and I thank her for that. I also benefited from good conversations at Young's with Paula Salvio.

I would also like to thank Michael DePorte, chair of the English department at UNH, and the Personnel Committee for granting me a course reduction in Spring 1996, which was crucial for me to write this book. An early grant from the Liberal Arts office helped me begin to use Goffman's performative theory in a paper on writing conferences, which prepared the way.

My association with Heinemann/Boynton Cook over the past fifteen years has been consistently gratifying. I want to thank Toby Gordon for her support and patience as I found a focus for the book. She is a truly superb editor. I also want to thank Scott Mahler for taking on the book in the latter stages of writing. His encouragement meant a lot to me. Finally, thanks to Vicki Kasabian for her expert work overseeing the production of the book.

I want to thank Donald Murray for his support of my work over the years (as well as for introducing me to college hockey). I want to thank my parents, who think everything I write is great. And to my family, Beth, Sarah, Abby, Andy, and Jackie, for reminding me of what's really important. Sarah, now in college, became a sounding board for some of the ideas in the book, and I truly enjoyed our talks.

Finally, I want to thank the many students whom I have taught in my Freshman English sections at the University of New Hampshire. I hope this book conveys my admiration for their work and my attempt to understand it.

Prologue

For years I have watched the arrival of freshmen at the University of New Hampshire where I teach. The streets of Durham are suddenly gridlocked with traffic backed up to the intersection a mile outside of town. Minivans, packed to the gills, inch toward the dormitories where they will double-park, triple-park, and begin to unload. The banks in town erect canopies, and soon lines form there too for checking accounts and ATM cards. U-Haul trailers appear in the parking lot with crude signs for refrigerators, futons, and unvarnished bookcases.

But for the past few years I have watched the ways parents and children behave on this day of parting. It all seems so awkward. The son or daughter in limbo, suspended between parents about to leave and friendships (they hope) about to begin. The parents running through details about settling in, trying to be helpful. "Do you know where you pick up your ID?" "You're going to need a fan, aren't you. We can go down to the discount store to get a cheap one." I see them standing, embarrassed, outside Burger King or the Bagelry, not making eye contact, a last meal before saying goodbye. And although these goodbyes are private, I have read about them often in papers students wrote early in September.

This year it was my turn. My wife and I made the two-car caravan to my daughter Sarah's school. When I first saw her room (naturally on the fourth floor), I was stunned by its smallness, made even smaller by the fact that her two roommates had arrived, and had taken up floor space with boxes and suitcases. I felt suddenly claustrophobic; I imagined the grinding proximity of this living space.

Students had been told that they should not unpack because they were immediately going on various camping trips, but Sarah's roommates had claimed desks, bookcases; they had left her with the upper bunk of the bed. There was no great advantage to claims her roommates had made, yet in this space each small territorial decision seemed magnified. Again, I had been here before, in student papers—arriving late and finding the room already arranged; the quiet anxiety, the sense that things have not started out right.

I was happy to make the repeated trips to the car and climb the four flights. This felt like useful work. It also kept me out her impossibly crowded room. My wife had cleared a place on the couch, and was reviewing, it seemed for the tenth time, plans for keeping in touch, the fact we'd be up for parents' day, encouragement to Sarah to come back any weekend she felt like it. . . . The car empty, I stood by the door, as awkward as the parents I had seen in Durham. And now it seemed as if I had crawled inside one of my students' papers. I'd been here dozens of times before. This was the moment, the threshold experience, with the quiet father by the door, out of reasons to hang around, about to say good-bye. I had become a cliché, but one that was intensely real. The good-bye. The hug. The walk down those stairs, feeling not helpless, but now unable to help.

I vowed to take these papers more seriously.

My initial purpose in this book was to clarify my appreciation of the personal writing students do. To do this I had to doubt much of what I knew, or thought I knew. I had to look again at the kinds of papers that persist no matter how much of E. B. White and Annie Dillard I have my students read. To engage in this clarification I have posed the following questions:

- What if we viewed "being personal" not as some natural "free" representation of self, but as a complex cultural performance?
- What does it take to perform this self successfully in a school context?
- What aesthetic of self-presentation do we promote?
- What literary sources do we draw on in creating this aesthetic?
- When students write about themselves in ways that seem unsuccessful (e.g., trite, superficial, sentimental) to us, are they drawing on forms of authoritative discourse the university seeks to stigmatize?
- Can we read against our own aesthetic to discover the power of papers we might initially dismiss?

These questions can help illuminate the ideological and literary roots of our own preferences; they can expose our own sense of "quality" as arbitrary, time-bound, culture-bound, and yes, class-bound. Student papers can provide a window onto discourses that hold power in the wider culture but not in the university. They can, I believe, also illuminate the alienation of the English Department culture from the mainstream of American life.

In this discussion I will occasionally use *we* to describe what I see as common teacher readings of student writing. I base these observations on years of work with teaching staffs. I also feel that in a very general way those who teach writing share some aesthetic principles which in this book I will call modernist. Yet I know how illusive any consensus on student writing can be, and therefore invite the reader to withdraw from that *we* at any time.

The book is structured into three sections. The first presents the central premise of the book, that writing is a performance of self, and it looks at one of the forms of performance—what I call the "turn"—that is one favored position. The second section forms the core of the book; it explores forms of self-performance that are out of favor in the academic culture, though they retain force in the wider culture.

In the final section, I directly engage the critics of expressivism, and by extension the place of personal writing. I hope my defense, though, will move beyond the polarized and sterile debate that has been the norm so far. I borrow heavily from the cultural studies perspective of these critics in trying to locate students in *literary* traditions, often juxtaposing their work with canonical literary texts. The traditional "God terms" of the writing process movement—"voice," "honesty," "truth telling"—have obscured this cultural situatedness.

Yet at the same time I hope to show that the cultural studies approach, as it has been applied to composition, has failed to acknowledge the moral power and utility of some of the discourses our culture makes available to students. Too often the student is seen as a pawn of inimical, capitalist-bred, media-purveyed discourse in which all that is bad in our society is encoded and endorsed. The composition teacher then rescues the student by providing defensive strategies of analysis. This view understates what I see as the moral power, energy, and self-confidence that is admirable in student writing, and in the students themselves.

1

Writing as Self-Presentation

If I had written to seek the world's favor, I should have bedecked myself better, and should present myself in a studied posture. I want to be seen here in my simple, natural, ordinary, fashion, without pose or artifice; for it is myself I portray.

—Montaigne, *Essays*

Everyone is discreet in confession.

—Montaigne, *Essays*

I have always ridiculed the false ingenuousness of Montaigne, who, while pretending to confess his defects, is careful to attribute to himself only such as are amiable.

—Jean-Jacques Rousseau, *Confessions*

My first teaching assignment, one for which I was woefully unprepared, was at Boston Trade High School in the Roxbury section of the city. The school looked like an abandoned factory with wire mesh on the windows and a heating system that took until mid-Tuesday to kick into gear. Many of the African American students had been born in the South, and some retained a drawl that subjected them to constant ridicule from their northernized peers. The school had the lowest reading level in the city, an astronomical dropout rate, and a constant level of disruption and petty intimidation.

I had, of course, seen too many movies where some idealistic teacher came into schools like this one, and after a few tough moments won the students over. It didn't happen that way for me. I felt at sea in a culture I didn't understand, unable to make even the most basic decisions (What do I do when a student calls me "Mr. Thing"? Laugh? Reprimand?). In retrospect, some of my misinterpretation is comical.

I remember once when a pair of students started "playing the dozens" (a term I learned much later).

"Yo mama's ugly. So ugly she won't die. She just ugly away."

"Well, yo mama's not ugly at all. She real cute. *We* had us a *nice* time."

Was this funny? Was this serious? It escalated, stopping just short of something violent, though that may have happened after school. At the end of class, I went up to one of the players who was still obviously upset and said, "I wouldn't take it seriously. I'm sure he doesn't even know your mother." He just looked at me like I was the stupidest person on earth.

My successes that first year were modest. I found my ninth graders loved to be read to; their favorite book was Claude Brown's *Manchild in the Promised Land,* which I read through twice. I also had some luck getting them to write. One of my freshmen, Kevin, even kept a journal on his own for several weeks. On the cover of his booklet he'd written "Kevin's Notebook—All Good Stories." And they were.

Kevin was big, almost sixteen, and the fastest talker I had every heard. He could hold the floor in a loud and active group—after the first Ali-Frazier fight, he took up the whole class time with his analysis. His written stories had the same breathless quality of his talk. Here is one he titled "Stories About a Girl I Met."

> The girl name is Linda she is Twenty one she have a Baby about four or five she digs me very much. I seen her last week she called me over across the street like something was happening Quit [Quite] natural I went over to see her i hadn't seen her in a month she just went crazy over me I know I am cool and all. But I didn't really care about her hugging and kissing me She know I have three diamond Rings But I don't think that's the Reason. she thinks my father own Hunts potato Chip Company that may be the reason she gave me her phone number I did not ask her for it But when I call her she is gone on a three weeks vacation out of town Now she will be back next week i wont to take her out to Dinner and to a movie somewhere Maybe to see No Place to Be somebody or something good. the end.

Though I liked Kevin's story, it was unlike the stories I was taught to write in school. It felt like an oral performance. Like all of his stories it moves at such a breathless clip that there is no time for much elaboration (e.g., what did Linda look like?) or even for punctuating sentences, as if any mark to slow down would risk losing the floor.

And I must admit that I was puzzled about how much of this really happened. A sexually mature twenty-one-year-old woman throwing herself all over a sixteen-year-old freshman, "going crazy" right there on the street? Where would he come up with money for dinner and expensive theatre tickets? Now I'm convinced that this fact/fiction line is irrelevant to what he was doing. This was a performance, maybe a kernel of fact, extended with wish fulfillment and a mild form of sexual boasting. If we ask, "Did this happen?" we miss the point.

My point of departure in this book is that all forms of "self-expression," all of our ways of "being personal" are forms of performance, in Erving Goffman's terms, "a presentation of self." The key feature of these presentations is their selectivity; every act of self-presentation involves the withholding of information that might undermine the idealized impression the performer wants to convey. For example, a presidential candidate in a debate must show a sincere desire to communicate with voters, as if he is loving every minute on the stage. In 1992 George Bush undermined this image when he glanced at his watch ("When will this thing be over?") near the end of the debate.

Goffman seeks to undermine the traditional concept of the autonomous self (a more recent target of the social constructionist). He writes:

> In our society the character one performs and one's self are somehow equated, and this self-character is usually seen as something housed within the body of the possessor, especially in the upper parts thereof . . . (1959, 252)

Evidence for this image of the "self" is everywhere—the way, for instance, we hold our hand over our heart, one possible location of this identity core, when we say the Pledge of Allegiance. There is Polonius' advice in *Hamlet*: "To thine own self be true; And it must follow, as night the day, thou canst not then be false to any man" (I.iii). When I first read *Hamlet* in high school, this was a line to be remembered and stored for graduation speeches and college applications, as if doddering Polonius had a flash of existential insight. It now seems so fatuous. Where is this unified self, this touchstone, Hamlet could consult? Isn't he caught in an ill-defined situation where he must pick between competing performative roles—father's son, mother's son, prince, lover, and student?

Perhaps the most grandiose claim for our capacity to reveal a self in writing comes in the opening chapter from the opening book of Jean-Jacques Rousseau's *Confessions*, written in 1767:

> I am commencing an undertaking, hitherto without precedent, and which will never find an imitator. I desire to set down before my fellows the likeness of a man in all the truth of nature, and that man myself.
>
> Myself alone! I know the feelings of my heart, and I know men. I am not made like any of those I have seen; I venture to believe that I am not made like any of those in existence. If I am not better, at least I am different. Whether

Nature has acted rightly or wrongly in destroying the mould in which she cast me, can only be decided after I have been read. (2)

Rousseau then conjures up the vision of himself on the Day of Judgment, presenting his book to the Sovereign Judge, proclaiming the truth of this book:

I have shown myself as I was: mean and contemptible, good, high minded and sublime, according as I was one or the other. I have unveiled my inmost self even as Thou hast seen it, O Eternal Being. (2)

In this opening page of his *Confessions* Rousseau makes several claims about self-expression:

- He is a distinct self, significantly unlike any man who has ever existed.
- Through an act of extraordinary frankness he can represent that self with complete honesty, "in all the truth of Nature."
- This book is so completely truthful that to read it is to read Rousseau himself. Book and man are so indistinguishable that God on Judgment Day need only read his book, all 680 pages of it.

As we read this opening, almost a quarter millennium after it was written, it seems to undermine its own claims. It is so clearly (and magnificently) a performance of self, with the self-conscious claims to sincerity (what Simon Schama [1989] calls "sensibilite") characteristic of the time. We hardly credit its claim to absolute distinctiveness, absolute honesty, even as we admire the writing. Some of Rousseau's effusions of feeling even make me uncomfortable —he claims an instant in-your-face intimacy that I'm not ready to grant. This is particularly the case with his novel *La Nouvelle Heloise*, a seemingly interminable collection of heartfelt letters that was the best-selling book in the eighteenth century. But to be fair Rousseau would very likely find the writing being done today at colleges and universities emotionally sterile.

According to Goffman, no one can be—or would want to be—as open as Rousseau claims to be. Who would want our idle judgments made public? We all rely on people to appear attentive when they are bored; to appear patient when they are in a hurry. We expect ballerinas to smile during the most complex turn and twirls. We expect authors to appear more smoothly knowledgeable in their books than they themselves feel when they write. As John Kenneth Galbraith once said, the spontaneity came into his writing on the fifth draft.

In short, in all public performances, from shaking hands to conducting a symphony, we selectively reveal ourselves in order to match an idealized sense of who we should be. This sense of idealization was beautifully illustrated in a scene from *The Wizard of Oz*, when Toto pulls the curtain aside to reveal a chubby old man speaking into a microphone; the impressive voice of the wizard was simply a product of amplification. In a last desperate gambit, the "wizard" warns, "Pay no attention to that man behind the curtain." We are to attend to the performance and not the man.

Even Goffman's (1959) term "presentation of self" suggests a distinction between "self" and "presentation" that he in fact dismantles in his discussion. We do not *have* a self that we selectively present, hiding *x*, revealing *y*. Rather the sense we have of being a "self" is rooted in a sense of competence primarily, but not exclusively, in social interaction. It is a sense of effectiveness, the robust feeling that we possess a repertoire of performances so natural that they cease to seem like performances at all. Our competence as social beings comes, in large measure, not from following Polonius' advice but from successfully internalizing the idealized models of who we should be. We feel this competence under attack when our performative routines fail us, in a foreign or hostile setting when we have difficulty "reading" the situation.

Goffman's performative theory has obvious analogues in rhetorical theory, particularly the concept of *ethos*. According to Quntilian the rhetorician must "possess, *and be regarded as possessing,* genuine wisdom and excellence of character" (Corbett 1971, emphasis added). Aristotle, though ambivalent about nonrational appeals, observed that the ethical appeal is exerted when the speech impresses the audience that the speaker is a person of sound sense, high moral character, and benevolence (Corbett 1971, 93). Although classical theorists, particularly Quintilian, insist that the speaker needs to truly *possess these virtues,* he also has to engage in what Goffman would call "impression management." Corbett writes:

> The *whole* of the discourse must maintain the "image" that the speaker seeks to establish. The ethical appeal, in other words must be pervasive throughout the discourse. The effect of the ethical appeal might very well be destroyed by a single lapse from good sense, good will, or moral integrity. A note of peevishness, a touch of malevolence, a flash of bad taste, a sudden display of inaccuracy or illogic could jeopardize a [speaker's] whole persuasive effort. (95)

This description echoes Goffman's claim that any public performance is, to a degree, treacherous; that there is the constant danger that "discrepant information" might invalidate a performance.

Another analogue would be Wayne Booth's (1961) concept of "implied author," developed in *The Rhetoric of Fiction*. Booth tried to sort out the issue of authorial presence in fiction; he is critical of the position of Ford Maddox Ford and others who claimed that the sentiments and values embodied in a work of fiction should be consistent with those held by the authors in their own lives (otherwise they would be insincere). According to Booth the author is not an unmediated presence in the work; instead he or she constructs an "implied author"—a distinct, "idealized" version of the autobiographical author, who establishes a scale of values in a work of fiction. He writes:

> A great work of fiction establishes the "sincerity" of its implied author, regardless of how grossly the man who created the author may belie in his *other* forms of conduct, the values embodied in the work. For all we know, the only sincere moments of his life may have been lived as he wrote the novel. (75)

Goffman allows us to extend the distinction Booth makes to virtually all forms of social interaction, including personal autobiographic writing. Here, too, a distinction can be made between a backstage, fragmented, autobiographical self and a "better," more unified version of self that we construct. The task for students, then, is not one of revelation but of construction. How to create a self that works, that will be taken seriously.

James Berlin has debunked this romantic version of freely exposing a "true self," which he claims is the false promise of expressivist classrooms:

> In this classroom, the student is asked to locate his or her private voice, innermost being, or authentic self. Emphasis is preeminently on freedom and self-expression. Peers in the class and the teacher, however, finally decide which of the student's various expressions of self is the "true" one, usually by indicating what is not "authentic" or "genuine" in the student texts read. The result is that the student's "true self" is subtly constructed by the responses of others in the class. The subject formation the student "finds" in the act of self-investigation and freely chooses as his or her "best" self is finally a construction of the classroom experience. (1996, 179)

Though Berlin moves from this position to advocate abandoning autobiographical writing in the composition class, his criticism also makes writing more interesting to speculate about. What kind of "self" are we inviting students to become? What kinds of "selves" do we subtly dismiss?

In this book I hope to show how Goffman's performative theory enables us to talk about student autobiographical writing in a new way, one that accounts more successfully for the ways we actually read and react. It reflects my own sense of frustration with the formalist tradition for evaluating writing, which presumed to isolate "qualities" of good writing as if they existed irrespective of content and blind to the cultural and ideological biases that inevitably came into play.

This formalist tradition, with its reliance on what Bob Connors (1994) has called "static abstractions," is as old as the field of composition itself; it is embodied in the first influential texts such as A. S. Hill's (1896) *The Foundations of Rhetoric* and Barrett Wendell's (1891) *English Composition* (the Strunk and White of the late nineteenth and early twentieth century). Hill identified "clearness," "force," "ease," and "unity" as central qualities. Wendell organized his text around two triads of terms. The first set—"unity," "mass," "coherence"—focused more on the organization and presentation of information. The second—clarity, elegance, and force—concerned the stylistics and the emotive power of writing. In the late fifties and early sixties, Paul Diederich (1974) of the Educational Testing Service developed a scale that could be used to evaluate the writing samples that would be built into the ETS's standardized tests. His four-item set of criteria for general merit—ideas, organization, wording, and flavor—are variants on the terms developed in the late nineteenth century.

These various scales often provide the comforting illusion that the qualities of good writing are something a piece of writing *has* and that our apprehension of these qualities equates to our reading experience. My own experience with these scales is that they fail to define what really happens, which is more subtle than any set of categories can depict. Terms like "ideas," "coherence," and "flavor" serve as cues to tacit expectations we have as readers, to an aesthetic sense we have developed. To the extent that readers of student work share this tacit aesthetic, this sense of perfomative expectation, it can appear that these categories are solid and explanatory. Paradoxically they are clear only if known, clear only if there is a shared substratum of experience and expectation. Yet to the outsider, the student unfamiliar with this aesthetic, "flavor" or "coherence" can be mystifying terms because students lack the set of tacit criteria the terms cue. Does mild profanity ("his course really sucked") provide flavor? How can they tell? What does it mean to write "honestly"? Honest in what way?

According to Goffman (1959), the key element of a socially competent performance is the ability to maintain a situation definition consistent with that of the audience. In these cases "honest" can cue a mutually agreed-upon type of performance. If definitions conflict, or if the situation appears ill-defined—often the case when students begin to write autobiographically—student writing can seem off the mark. I'll illustrate with the initial free writing from a recent first-year writing class.

In the first class I wanted students to write about some passion, obsession, some particular interest of competence that might set them apart from other students. To set the stage I read an excerpt from Charles Simic's (1994) wonderful essay, "Food and Happiness," which opens with scenes from his childhood in post-World War II Yugoslavia. The excerpt ended with a bean-eating contest (which Simic loses):

> We were eating on a big terrace watched by nosy neighbors who kept score. At some point, I remember, I just slid off my chair onto the floor.
>
> I'm dying, it occurred to me. My uncle was still wielding the spoon with his face deep in the plate. There was a kind of hush. . . . Finally even my uncle staggered off to bed and I was left alone, sitting under the table, the heat intolerable, and the sun setting, my mind blurry, thinking, This is how a pig must feel. (8)

Roger LaMarque responded by detailing his own obsession with his shortness:

> Since I was very young I would always climb. The refrigerator, the crib, the wall. It didn't matter. I don't know what it is that causes me to surmount an obstacle, but I think it is height. I've been small all my life. Even as I've grown to a height of 5'10" I am still seen as short or small. Maybe some psychological force drives me to see the top of heads I have never seen before. . . .
>
> I remember when I was younger, when my cousin D. was born. I went to see him but at that age he just seemed a blue crying mess. Three years later I saw him again. He was tottering around the house and as I walked by I realized that I could see the top of his head. The strangeness of this little before seen item astounded me. I felt I was missing out on a whole slice of life by being short. That night promptly led to me bowing down in front of a large wall mirror to view the top of my head. My hair kept flapping over, however, so I faced away from my mirror and leant back as far as I could, holding the mirror up to my face so that I could see the top of my head. My mother walked by and told me to get a haircut.

I was attracted to this self-introduction not simply because Roger used "specifics." I am attracted to the manner of self-presentation. His use of the word "maybe" suggests the tentative exploratory attitude of the essayist, creating the impression that the meaning is coming to him as he writes. I like the irony and self-mocking humor, in fact the way he seems to subvert any seriousness associated with my assignment. Others can write about their love of animals or music, he seems to say, I'll go with the tops of heads.

Other students approached this task of self-presentation in an entirely different way. Here is how one began:

> I would describe myself as an extremely caring person. It gives me a sense of well-being when I get a chance to do something for another person.

> I think my job as lifeguard is what started this passion. This is when I started to enjoy helping other people.

By this point I felt something had gone awry. In the first sentence, the expression "extremely caring person" made me think that the writer had not picked up the invitation in the way that I had hoped. I feel like I am about to drown in sincerity. At the same time I am troubled by my reaction—how could this writer have known my tacit agenda? The Simic excerpt was hardly enough of a cue. And why am I so put off by her focus on the sincerity of her moral commitment to others? Clearly she has identified a more significant feature of her life than Roger has.

It is even possible to shift the situation slightly and see this as a very effective way of showing oneself. Suppose this were not a paper for an English class, but an interview for admission to the UNH Occupational Therapy program (which is, in fact, her major). I suspect that in that context her sincerity, her lack of cleverness, would work to her credit.

As I thought about my reaction, I remembered a comment made by a freshman in a study of differences between student and instructor reactions to four papers. In commenting on one of the papers that dealt with a student's obsession for getting mail, the student said that it had "the tone of an English paper." I asked what he meant:

> She's taking something that seems menial to people and she's making it a big deal. And I think they [English teachers] like to see that. I think they like to see students write about something like a tree and make it flowery, make it come alive. So I think they would like "Mailaholic" because its no big deal to get mail and she made it sound like it was really something. She talks about different characteristics and stuff. (Newkirk 1984, 306)

In other words English teachers operate on a principle of inversion, expecting students to magnify the menial, as Roger seems to do, to subvert the conventional evaluation of significance. Is that at the heart of my reaction? And how could a student possibly know that?

My French teacher in college once told the story of a schoolboy in a very traditional French school. One day this boy went up to the headmaster, a dignified man with a long beard.

"Excuse me, sir, I'd like to ask you a question."

The headmaster answered brusquely, "Well, what is it?"

"When you sleep, sir, do you put your beard above or below the covers?"

"What nonsense is this? Get on to your class."

A couple days later, the headmaster, now looking a little haggard, spots the boy on the school yard, comes up to him and begins to shake him, "You wretch, on account of you I've lost two nights' sleep!"

It can be unsettling to penetrate the habitual, to disturb the "normal." But I hope to show it can be freeing as well. Reading against the grain of our own (or *my own*) preferences can illuminate the roots of these preferences. Mina Shaughnessy taught a generation of composition teachers to see student writing as logical and plausible. Working among boxes of old placement essays, with sentences that violate every grammatical sensibility, she showed the intelligence behind the sentence gone awry. I hope to do something similar with autobiographical writing.

For it is easy to dismiss so much of what students write as trivial, sentimental, shallow, platitudinous, and clichéd. Last year my daughter, in the midst of writing her application essays, shared with me a handout entitled, "Danger: Sleepy Prose Ahead (or, The Sandman Cometh)." I'll quote a short section on the "Jock" essay to convey the tone:

> Musicians, actors, lab interns, yearbook editors, club officers—students from every walk of high school life have succumbed to the questionable charms of the Jock essay, flocking like doomed ducks to a wooden decoy. Still, though, scholar-athletes sound its most familiar and resonant note: "Through wrestling I have learned to set goals, to go all out, and to work with people." Now *that's* a frightening prospect.

True enough, I am not moved or even greatly convinced by sentences like this one—although, having lived with wrestlers, I know something of their dedication and sense of fraternity. But I cringe at the hostility of this advice-giver. *Why does this sentence provoke this reaction in us? What aesthetic sensibility does it violate so profoundly that we compare the writer to a "doomed duck"?* Could it be a distaste for such a sweaty sport as wrestling? Would our reaction be the same if the sentence began, "Through my work in the theatre . . ."? What is the source of this profound irritation?

By reading sentences like this one against the grain, I try to imagine a context in which it can be significant and meaningful—even admirable.

2

The Turn

We look for the sermon in the suicide, for the social or moral lesson in the murder of five. We interpret what we see, select the most workable of multiple choices. We live entirely, especially if we are writers, by the imposition of a narrative line upon disparate images, by the "ideas" with which we have learned to freeze the shifting phantasmagoria which is our actual experience.

—Joan Didion, *The White Album*

In *Fragments of Rationality* (1992), Lester Faigley questions the extent of the "freedom" offered to students in classes that stress personal writing:

> The freedom students are given in some classes to choose and adapt auto-biographical assignments hides the fact that these same students will be judged by the teachers' unstated assumptions about subjectivity and that every act of writing they perform occurs within complex relations of power. (128)

Faigley reminds us that the invitation to write about a significant life event is hardly the open and innocent invitation that it appears to be—for we as teachers have criteria, often unstated, for the kind of subjectivity that we will take seriously. Even if we avoid grading, even if we confine ourselves to the role of supportive coach and editor, we can't escape our own patterns of gratification. This chapter explores a popular genre of personal writing, the personal essay, by looking at the way students are implicitly invited to present themselves. It begins with "the paper from hell" reproduced in Robert Connors' (1996) essay, "Teaching and Learning as a Man."

The student essay, ghoulishly titled "Horsing Around," describes an increasingly reckless hunting adventure with two friends. They begin by shooting a crow; first, the friend with a .22, then the author, blasting the dead bird into "about twelve pieces" with a shotgun. Next they wander into a field where a horse trotted toward them. The author's friend Jim dared him to shoot:

> Without thinking of the seriousness involved, I raised the gun to my shoulder, took careful aim, and KABOOM! I nailed him in the left hindquarter

11

and he let out a yelp like a dog getting his tail sliced off. At first I thought I might have killed the animal, but I was too afraid to stick around to find out. All I remember hearing after I shot the gun was the horse yelping and Bill shouting; going into hysterics about what I had done.

They hurry back to the jeep, and in the original draft the story ends as follows:

> While in the jeep, Jim was laughing so hard that he wet his pants. We finished up our unusual and impromptu hunting excursion by cleaning the guns and drinking more beer.

The "subjectivity" displayed in this narrative was (understandably) not acceptable to the teacher. The reason is not simply the cruelty of the action described, but that there is no reflexive move on the part of the author to recognize that cruelty. He ends the essay at the same level of moral (in)sensitivity that he began. The recollection and rendering of the experience did not lead to any redeeming insight that might provide a kind of atonement for the act. Consequently the teacher encouraged the author to add a paragraph in which he talked about the theme of the paper. The new ending went as follows:

> Looking back now, the whole thing seems pretty funny, but I also regret it. I feel bad about hurting the horse and I think the incident probably wouldn't have happened if it hadn't been for the combination of boredom, beer, and boyhood.

This ending is hardly convincing; a great many bored young men manage to drink and not shoot horses for fun. One also wonders about the sincerity of this conclusion, given the fact that he keeps the original title, "Horsing Around." Yet the author begins to use some of the expected conventions of the confessional personal narrative. He has constructed two time positions: a self that commits the act, and an older "wiser" self that looks back to judge that action. We are asked to believe that this act of looking back has created a chastened and morally more sensitive individual. Faigley would argue that this new ending shows the author's understanding of power relations in personal writing, the expectation that experiences be rendered as moral lessons.

In order to construct this subjectivity, the student writer needs to negotiate convincing "turns" in the writing, shifts from rendering to reflection that point to the "significance" (a key word in personal essay assignments) of the experience being rendered. It is a way of dealing with the "so what?" question—what meaning does this have for a reader? Frequently this reflection does not reveal any startlingly new insight; we don't "learn" about mortality from reading "Once More to the Lake." Rather, the effect comes from the way the insight is "earned" and dramatized from an examination of experience. The personal essay dramatizes thought by showing the writer as someone open to the potentially transforming effects of a life sensitively encountered. Even confessions of inadequacy, insensitivity, and cruelty are redeemed by those reflexive turns that show the writer has—often, it seems, through the act of writing itself—achieved a measure of self-understanding and moral growth.

The paradigmatic example of this form of self-presentation is George Orwell's "Shooting an Elephant," an essay which bears an eerie resemblance to "Horsing Around." The majority of the essay, as almost any freshman knows, is taken up with an account of Orwell tracking down and killing an elephant that had run wild in a Burmese village. Woven into this compelling account Orwell reflects upon the significance of the event he describes, placing it in a wider frame of meaning:

> One day something happened which in a roundabout way was enlightening. It was a tiny incident itself, but it gave me a better glimpse than I had before of the real nature of imperialism—the real motives for which despotic governments act. ([1936] 1988, 769)

In effect, he promises us an essay, one that will move ("turn") from the local or "tiny" to the general.

With two thousand Burmese villagers behind him eager for a shooting, Orwell realizes why he must follow though with what is now a pointless killing:

> And it was at that moment, as I stood there, with the rifle in my hands, that I first grasped the hollowness, the futility, of the white man's dominion in the East. Here was I, the white man with his gun, standing in front of the unarmed native crowd—seemingly the leader of the piece; but in reality I was only the absurd puppet pushed to and fro by the will of those yellow faces behind. I perceived in this moment that when the white man turns tyrant it is his own freedom he destroys. (771)

This turn does a number of things:

- It creates a "before and after" moment that is dramatically satisfying. This was not an understanding arrived at slowly; it is represented as flash of realization, an epiphany arrived at in a moment of extreme psychological pressure.
- It provides thematic weight to the essay. It allows us to consider a major issue, the motives for oppressive action in colonial governments, through his examination of this "tiny" event.

- It illustrates a mind at work, moving from particular to general, making sense of experience. It is therefore a model of learning, an illustration of what John Dewey called "intelligence."
- The essay has a confessional urgency. Orwell is "guilty" of a sin that is expiated in the writing. The reader senses a personal need to confess not only to the killing itself, but to the racism bred by colonialism. This willingness to reveal something disagreeable enhances Orwell's "ethical" appeal—here is a man willing to show himself at his worst.
- It shows the writer moving to higher moral ground. The early Orwell, young and "poorly educated," plays the role of oppressor without knowing why. The Orwell that emerges from this experience is more conscious of motivation and more capable of opposing the colonialist system. The act of writing the essay itself shows Orwell now to be a formidable opponent of colonialism.

Something like this pattern operates in many of the most widely anthologized essays—Hoagland's "The Courage of Turtles," Ephron's "Growing Up Absurd," White's "Once More to the Lake." These essays dramatize learning, they illustrate the possibility of personal growth, and they celebrate, indirectly, the heuristic power of writing itself. *Writing is the hero of the writing.*

As readers we sense the possibility of writing to break through conventional representation; it is the sensation writers so often talk about—the writer listening to the emerging text for instruction, a "wise receptiveness" that Donald Murray (1989) in one book title has called, paradoxically, "expecting the unexpected."

> The reason I write is simple: to surprise myself.
>
> I want to discover what I know that I didn't know I knew, to see a familiar subject in an unfamiliar way, to contradict my most certain beliefs, to burst through expectation and intent to insight and clarity, to hurt and laugh, understand and be confused in a way that I had not experienced before. (47)

This is more than advice for writing. It is an invitation to construct the self in a particular way; a self in a state of "suspended conclusion," open to change, with everything—even our "most certain beliefs"—on the table. This self is malleable, not exactly fluid, but open to the transformative moments that can occur when experience is contemplated in the relative tranquility of writing. Murray defines what Faigley calls a "subjectivity," and what I will term an "ideology of the self," a form of self-presentation that will be taken seriously by the reader.

The ideological basis of this view of writing can be shown by pitting it against other strongly held beliefs about selfhood. At a recent meeting of the Conference on Composition and Communication, I attended a session that focused on a student paper written by a young lay minister in an introductory writing class. The assignment was to analyze Richard Rodriguez' *Hunger of Memory* using Mary Louise Pratt's critical concept of "contact zones" (1991). The writer found the book reprehensible because Rodriguez showed such profound disrespect for his parents, a violation of one of the Ten Commandments; in fact, he became so angry that midway through he began referring to the author as a "punk." The teacher, apparently, was pushing the student to try to understand Rodriguez' point of view, to invite some empathy for his need to pull away. I suspect she was seeking one of those "I've come to see . . ." moments of sympathetic extension. But the student resisted this invitation, adding only a few perfunctory sentences at the end of the paper—though he eventually admitted that as a Christian it was his duty to "forgive" Rodriguez.

I suspect that a student with this form of Christian conviction would find Murray's advice either mystifying or actually blasphemous. Why would anyone invite an experience that "contradicted" basic beliefs? How could a profound and unconditional belief possibly be so open to change and contradiction? Experience is the living out of a commitment and a promise, not the perpetual calling into question of these basic beliefs. From this standpoint, the "self" Murray describes would be capricious, ungrounded, unstable, and dangerously secular. For this student, and for many evangelical Christians, the college writing class is a foreign place where they often find that their most personal writing is treated as unreflective and dogmatic.

My point is not to dwell on the problem of evangelical Christians in the writing class (though I feel that is a topic that deserves more sensitive attention than it has been given). I simply want to stress that Murray's vision, and the claims of the personal essay, often rest on a view of the self as fundamentally changeable, in fact eager to shed more than a skin.

Earning an Insight

Although I want to raise some questions about what I perceive as the dominance of the personal essay as a meaning-making genre, like most composition teachers I am deeply gratified when the turn is graceful and convincing. In this section I look at two quite different examples. The first, called "One More Stepping Stone," adopts the conventions of the recovering addict's "confession." It begins:

> In the harshest of terms I am a recovering drug addict. In the best light I was an immature girl experimenting. I lean toward the first assessment. Being heavily addicted to marijuana was my first mistake. The second was cocaine, to which I was not heavily addicted, but enjoyed a little too much and too often.

The author establishes a double perspective early in the essay contrasting the "self" that became addicted with the recovering "self" writing the paper. For example, she gives us two "takes" on Edward, the young man who introduced her to drugs:

> Edward, oh what visual images are conjured up by that word. He was exactly the kind of guy I thought I fancied. Dressed in black combat boots, ripped flannels and jeans, he was holding his sketchbook as if it were the world's most valuable possession. Long blond locks escaped his ponytail. His ice blue eyes were intriguing and inviting. I could not resist them. His face revealed a lost and scared child inside all this rough tough exterior.

She follows immediately with a countervision:

> Now, years later, when I think of Edward I see a little misguided, scared and scary drug addict. I realize how greasy his hair is and how nauseating his clothes smell. I feel sorry for the loss of such potentially great artwork. I feel sorry for him throwing his life into a little plastic bag.

She details her growing use of marijuana, her loss of virginity with Edward at a drug dealer's house, a "five minute episode that creates more regret in me than I could ever put into words." And her casual use of cocaine:

> Doing cocaine never became a habit. It was kind of like Godiva chocolate; if anybody had some, I'd love a little bit.

The turning point, what she calls "the night of infamy," came at another party when her cousin asked her if she wanted to shoot up:

> My reply was yes. I shot up heroin and after seeing everything whirl around me like dripping paint, I passed out.
>
> The next day I woke up feeling different. I looked at all the people from the previous night who, like me, ended up sleeping there because there was no way to get home. I looked at them and almost threw up in my bed. Some were already smoking pot again, some were drinking, and others were looking for cocaine. One in particular had vomit all over his clothes, a bloody arm, and could not walk straight. He was looking for some lines of cocaine. I looked to my left arm and found proof that I was in too deep. I was repulsed by the entire scene.

This experience triggers her decision to stop using drugs and leads to her not-surprising conclusion:

> Above and beyond all this, I know myself! I know who I have been and who I can be. I do not know what path to take to find my dreams, but I know which one I will avoid. We all have different stepping stones on our life path. I got over one of mine.

This ending, looked at in isolation, may seem highly conventional. She uses a commonplace of life as composed of strategic and necessary challenges—indeed she writes that "in a way I am glad it all happened." Because she has to deal with this challenge she knows her own potential for making bad judgments. Yet I would argue it is "earned" because of the way she has shown, with great candor and no self-pity, the process of her infatuation and degradation, leading to a climactic scene, which she renders in effective detail. The scene is the formal equivalent of Orwell shooting the elephant, the moment of epiphany, when she confronts her growing addiction. This conclusion, though it says nothing "new," arises convincingly out of the narrative that proceeded it.

The second piece makes the turn in a different way, self-consciously avoiding a conventional reaction to the event described. In "The Window," Roger LaMarque (who in Chapter 1 uses a mirror to look at the top of his head) describes a window at the base of a stairway in his dorm, which looks out on an open courtyard. It is in that courtyard that two homeless vagrants in Durham live. Roger describes his experience of looking out through that window at the blankets the men had left there:

> I felt like I was ten, with my face pressed up against the thick glass at the Roger Williams Zoo. I felt like I was standing on the thin concrete border, face pressed eagerly against the cold plate waiting for a polar bear to swim by and press his paw against the window so I could press my hand back and turn and laugh with my mother at the size difference. I remember the people used to be disappointed when they weren't in the water so that we could watch them.
>
> Standing there, looking under the building, I wondered when the men would come to sleep. The window made it so easy to look out there and imagine the blankets being used. The window made it almost like television, where it would be resolved in an hour, but only if you watched. The physical barrier took away all the power of the place, and made it a place where bums slept. No longer was it real, but it was outside and I was in. It was a hard feeling to shake.

> I don't know the history of the human race real well. I don't know when we started making separations among ourselves, but I would guess it happened when some of us moved inside. We could look out from our caves and see the outside without being there. I don't think we realize how strong that power is. We are able to witness that which occurs, without playing a part or affecting the outcome. We have it brought to us, without risk, without thought.

To appreciate the subtlety of this "turn," it is useful to imagine the more conventional response he might have given. The situation obviously calls up guilt, outrage, a feeling of helplessness, questions about how this could happen in "the richest nation of earth," perhaps a reflection on what the writer might do (e.g., donate time or money to the homeless shelter in Portsmouth). These are, as I have tried to argue, morally admirable responses that we need to respect despite their lack of originality. But for me at least, Roger's turn exhibits the particularizing vision we expect from the essay, a perspective Roger established in the sentences before the section I have quoted. He distinguishes his own experience with the homeless from the more conventional images:

> I didn't see homeless men huddling for warmth near a burning barrel of garbage. I didn't get spotted by a drunken man, nor was I yelled at for staring at homeless people. But I felt guilty. I'm not pressing a social statement, nor making excuses for national or personal guilt. I simply felt guilty.

The purpose of this move is to self-consciously distance himself from the typical guilt-inducing images, and to announce a particularized perspective—he is saying, "I'm not trying to make a social statement, I'm just trying to understand my own guilt." But as he moves on to the next paragraph, with his wonderful image of the swimming polar bear, his theme becomes clearer—*he feels guilty because he can remain detached.* The dorm window, and variants on this window (e.g., television, the glass, the zoo), "took away the power of the place."

Roger takes on the "subjectivity" that the personal essay presupposes. The experience he writes about, looking out at a courtyard with blankets in it, lacks the overt dramatic power of being confronted by a drunk (as Roger reminds us). It seems small at first, yet it serves as the vehicle for a thoughtful meditation on the roots of indifference. The self "presented" in the essay is one open to the transformative potential of even "minor" experiences. Or as it was put more cynically by a student quoted earlier, it's the capacity to make a "big deal" out of something small, a characteristic of English teachers, who in the minds of students, see "symbols" everywhere.

The essay is also "transgressive." The essayist is acutely alert to conventional event-response patterns (see homeless people → express guilt and a desire to make a difference). They know there is no real mileage in staying within the expected. They refuse to play it straight. As I recall Roger, slouching in class, still worn out and bruised from the previous day's rugby practice, wearing his sunglasses in our dim windowless class, he would much rather fail in an unexpected way than succeed according to the rules he knew too well.

The Critique of the Personal Essay

When students are invited to write about "significant" events in their lives, writing teachers read about the full range of trauma—divorce, child abuse, eating disorders and other addictions, dysfunctional families, loneliness, deep unhappiness. Recently critics of the personal essay have objected that students' privacy is invaded when they are expected to disclose such intimate information. While it is possible that an insensitive teacher could establish "disclosure" as a tacit criteria, I have been impressed by how rarely this seems to happen. Over the past two decades I have read thousands of anonymous, student-written evaluations of teachers in our program. I cannot remember one in which a student made this kind of complaint. The overwhelming and consistent comments we see are those of appreciation for the opportunity to write and reflect on life experiences. I suspect that opponents of the personal essay may appear to "protect" students from this "invasion"—one that is not experienced by students themselves—in order to advance another teaching agenda.

Another obvious criticism of "allowing" this type of writing is that it forces us to assume a role of therapist. Underlying this criticism is one questionable assumption—that when students write on these topics, they *want* us to assume a counseling role. In most cases, this represents a profound and presumptuous misreading of student intent. Paradoxically, these writing situations can be therapeutic precisely because we don't act as therapists. If the first response is "I can't respond to this as a piece of writing because it is so personal. Have you thought about talking to a counselor?" we are denying the student the "normal" role of writer. The experience is stigmatized, it is represented to the student as outside the bounds of normal classroom discourse. The student who may have spent considerable time and energy on the writing sees it confined into a strange category—writing that can't be treated as writing ("I really can't *grade* this.")

In fact, the therapeutic power of such writing may be the experience of having it treated as "normal"—that is, writing that can be responded to, critiqued, even graded. Writing may have healing power because it represents a *third* part of the relationship; it is an artifact, a construction, a relatively stable representation of experience. By asking many of the most basic conferencing questions—those that encourage elaboration, reflection, and the exploration of other perspectives—I believe we can respond sympathetically and helpfully. Paradoxically, the writing can most effectively be therapeutic by not being *directly* therapeutic.

A third kind of criticism focuses on the implicit ideology of the personal essay. Lester Faigley (1992) claims that the personal essay is not the natural, freely chosen, "authentic," seemingly universal form of expression that advocates of personal writing claim it is. Instead, it is a "socially and historically specific discursive practice" (128); and when students are asked to write personally, they are subjects of "an institutional exercise of power" (131). The assignment to write a personal essay invites students to make a particular kind of performance, to assume a fairly specific form of "subjectivity." At this point Faigley seems to fall into a postmodern black hole. Because the personal essay is bounded in this way, he argues that the alternative is to encourage students to practice kinds of writing that "resist" dominant discourses. Yet one can easily imagine that as these discourses of resistance are rewarded in the classroom, they too are enmeshed in a power relationship.

I want to borrow part of Faigley's argument, though: if the personal essay is discursively bound, what are those boundaries? What is this preferred construction of self, and what problems might this "preference" raise for students? What subjectivities are ruled out?

Ambivalence About the Narrative. There is a strange schizophrenia about narrative writing in English departments. On the one hand they are built upon the narrative—it should come as no news that students become English majors to get academic credit for reading narrative fiction. Yet in writing classes there is the sense that narratives are relatively easy to write and academically suspect. Just looking at my bookshelf I find a title, *Writing Narrative—and Beyond* (Dixon and Stratta 1986), implying that the "beyond" is more advanced and sophisticated. (Imagine if the title were *Writing Narrative and Below.*) This suspicion of narrative affects the way the narrative component of student essays is treated.

If the student is viewed as "making meaning" in the personal essay, and *if* this act of meaning making is seen as the movement—the turn—from the specific (narrative) to the thematic (commentary), it follows that our work focuses on this move to claim thematic significance, to lift (there's that "beyond" again) the representation out of the particulars of experience. Take, for example, the way Orwell's "Shooting an Elephant" is presented in *The Norton Reader* Seventh Edition. It appears in the section, "Politics and Government," announcing the thematic orientation we are to take to an essay that is primarily a narrative. At the end of the essay the reader is asked questions which almost cause the narrative to disappear:

> What issue does Orwell address and what kind of evidence is proper to it? Does he prove anything?
>   Where does he state his thesis? Would it have been better to argue his thesis directly rather than mainly by example? (774)

The key word is "example." The narrative is almost completely subordinated to the thematic content of the essay, reduced to being an "example." This seems to me an instance of what Walker Percy calls the "loss of the creature," the way a propensity to generalize causes the "spoilation" of the particular which is "*disposed of* by theory":

> The tree loses its proper density and mystery as a concrete existent and, as merely another *specimen of* a species, becomes itself nugatory. ([1975] 1984, 89)

Orwell's dramatic account loses its proper density as our focus is directed to questions of empire.

Malleability of the Self. One common criticism of the personal essay is that it presumes a coherent "self," in Faigley's (1992) terms a "unified consciousness to be laid out on the page." I argue the exact opposite here. Essayists consistently deny this stability, beginning with Montaigne himself:

> Not only does the wind of accident move me at will, but besides, I am moved and disturbed as a result merely of my unstable posture; and anyone who observes carefully can hardly find himself twice in the same state. I give my soul now one face, now another, according to the direction I turn it. If I speak of myself in different ways, that is because I look at myself in different ways. All contradictions may be found in me by some twist and in some fashion. . . . [W]hoever studies himself really attentively will find in himself, yes, even in his judgment, this gyration and discord. I have nothing to say about myself absolutely, simply and solidly, without confusion and without mixture, or in one word. ([1580] 1957, 2: 242)

This proclamation of changeability is something of a pose. Although Montaigne's moods and interests change, there seems a consistent (and very appealing) persona—wise, learned, skeptical—that stabilizes his essays. But his statement does provide a cue to one form of self-presentation that will be taken seriously; the writer needs to present a malleable self, one that can be affected "significantly" by experience. The "self" is always at risk, in play, engaged in the process of growth and change. It can turn, even gyrate. To give it a name, this view is "developmental"; the writer is engaged in a staged process of self-actualization.

In other words, the essay, as students are often invited to write it, is a narrative of developmental progress. (Montaigne himself did not use the essay in this way—he was too much the skeptic to see his life as moving consistently in the direction of greater self-awareness.) Not only is it a progress narrative, but it is one that asks for a construction of experience in a particular dramatic form; it requires the capacity to identify critical disjunctive moments that trigger self-reflective growth (Orwell shooting the elephant; Roger at the window; Amy waking up after a night of heroin use). Growth is not incremental; it consists of a series of before-and-after experiences that result in qualitative change. Take, for example, some of the assignments from Coles and Vopat's (1985) *What Makes Writing Good:*

> What separates a child from an adult? (Janet Kotler)
>
> When was the last time you made an important choice in your life? (Irmscher)
>
> Choose a moment from your own experience or from that of someone you know in which a presumed limit was found not to exist. Describe the moment of discovery. (Robert Holland)
>
> I am asking you to write about a first or last experience. Since this is likely to be a memorable experience that has been of some consequence in your life, you will need to present it in the wider context of your life. (Sandra Schor)

I want to make clear that I like these assignments, and use similar ones in my own class. But I have become aware that each focuses on a disjunctive illuminating moment, a before-and-after experience that, once identified, enables the writer to achieve the dramatic developmental perspective expected in the personal essay.

There is also a strong moralistic dimension to this form, as there is to any confessional act. The writer emerges (or appears to emerge—or constructs an image of a self that emerges) from the essay as a more admirable, more self-aware, often more moral person. The Orwell that writes is not the unconscious racist who shot the elephant; the woman who emerges from her account of drug use is someone who can now make her own decisions. We judge these personal essays by how convincingly the writer demonstrates progressive movement along unstated lines of human development.

The personal essay, as I have tried to describe it, mirrors many of the values teachers hold—in effect, it invites students to see themselves as learners, open to revising even deeply held beliefs. It utilizes narrative conventions we admire in literature. And it celebrates the capacity of writing for self-examination and personal discovery. It may also pose difficulties for some students, and it may exclude a range of topics and self-presentations.

- Some students do not see their lives as hinging on key disjunctive moments. When I was discussing the ideas for this chapter with a college freshman, she said, "I'm eighteen. How many before-and-after moments am I supposed to have?" Students, with some justification, may see the invitation to discuss "significant" events as favoring those who have experienced some form of life trauma, no matter how much we insist that this is not the case.

- As noted earlier, some students see the "self" as relatively formed, and their experience as a working-out of deeply held convictions that they will not put at risk. They would find Montaigne's "gyrations" and Murray's claim that he hopes to "contradict his most certain beliefs" as pathological. As a result they cannot find a way to assume the tentative exploratory posture the essay invites.

- If students perceive the code word "significant" as restricting them to transformative events, a wide range of experience is excluded. I'm thinking particularly of those things students do that are habitual, pleasurable, comic, disrespectful, non-self-improving—when they drop the mask of the student.

Probably at no time in a student's life does this burden of appearing the serious learner weigh more heavily than in the writing of college application essays. What, for example, are they to make of the casual invitation on one application for one prestigious school:

> Please use the space on this page to let us know something about you that we might not know from the rest of your application. . . . There is no "correct" way to respond to the essay request. In writing about something that matters to you, you will convey to us a sense of yourself.

Any student that really believes this disclaimer does not merit admission.

One application essay has become an Internet classic, passed from student to student, each of whom remembered the time they had to labor to show the "significance" of their life experience. It was written to the familiar prompt:

In order for the admissions office staff of our college to get to know you, the applicant, better, we ask that you answer the following question: Are there any significant experiences you have had, or accomplishments you have realized, that helped define you as a person?

The student, Hugh Gallagher, answered as follows:

I am a dynamic figure, often seen scaling walls and crushing ice. I am known to remodel train stations on my lunch breaks, making them more efficient in the area of heat retention. I translate ethnic slurs for Cuban refugees, I write award-winning operas, I manage time efficiently. Occasionally I tread water for three days in a row.

It continues with a list of accomplishments ("Critics worldwide swoon over my original line of corduroy evening wear.") And he finishes as follows:

I balance, I weave, I dodge, I frolic, and my bills are all paid. On weekends, to let off steam, I participate in full-contact origami. Years ago I discovered the meaning of life but forgot to write it down. I have made extraordinary four course meals using only a mouli and a toaster oven, I breed prize-winning clams. I have won bullfights in San Juan, cliff-diving competitions in Sri Lanka, and spelling bees in the Kremlin. I have played Hamlet, I have performed open heart surgery, and I have spoken to Elvis.

But I have not gone to college.

In part this is a parody of the thirst colleges have for extracurricular activities. But I suspect the students e-mailing this essay across the country also enjoy the way Gallagher plays with the invitation to discuss "significant" experiences. To that request he seems to reply, "Yeah, I've done a few things, here and there. Nothing big. But the true transformative experience, dear admissions office, is yet to come. That will be the experience of going to your college."

According to my sources, he *was* admitted.

3

The Problem of Emotion

*In the second story, if you have not forgotten, huntsmen wound an
elk, she has the look of a human being, and no one has the heart to kill
her. Not a bad subject, but dangerous in this respect, that it is hard to
avoid sentimentality; the piece has to be written in the style of a police
report, without words that arouse pity, and should begin like this:
"On such and such a date huntsmen wounded a young elk in the
Daraganov forest." But should you moisten the language with a tear,
you will deprive the language of its sternness and of everything
deserving attention. . . .*

—Anton Chekhov

As memories of Michael Dukakis' failed presidential campaign fade, two
images remain. One is a photograph of Dukakis in the turret of a tank, wearing a helmet that made him look like Bullwinkle's sidekick, Rocky. The other
occurred during the second debate with George Bush. By this point Dukakis
was trailing and needed a strong performance to have any chance of winning.
That chance faded with his answer to the first question from Bernard Shaw:

Shaw: Governor, if Kitty Dukakis were raped and killed would you favor an
irrevocable death penalty for the killer?

Dukakis: No I don't, Bernard, and I think you know I've opposed the death
penalty all my life. I don't see any evidence that it's been a deterrent and
I think there are more effective [ways] of dealing with violent crime.
We've done so in my state and that's why we have the biggest drop in
crime of any industrial state in America. . . .

Dukakis' failure to express emotion at the prospect of his wife being raped and
killed helped confirm the view of many that he was a bloodless bureaucrat. The
account of the debate in *Time Magazine* might be taken as the *vox populi:*

> The question was in ghoulish taste, but it proved revealing. Moderator
> Bernard Shaw of CNN began the final debate by demanding that Dukakis
> reconcile his opposition to capital punishment with a macabre scenario in
> which his wife Kitty Dukakis was raped and killed. Such a hypothesis

25

justified almost any conceivable answer. Dukakis could have vented his anger at the premise of the question or passionately explained his own feeling of outrage. . . . But even as his political dreams hung in the balance, Dukakis mustered all the emotion of a time and temperature recording. (*Time*, October 24, 1988, 18)

I remember feeling out of step with this public reaction (as I did often in that campaign). Dukakis' answer seemed reasonable to me, even reassuring. He wasn't going to put on a show of emotion for Bernard Shaw; he wasn't going to fabricate a hypothetical thirst for vengeance, or even suggest that a belief he had held all his life would be called into question if his wife were raped and killed. I liked that steadiness. Yet this one failure to be openly passionate doomed his campaign.

Classical rhetoricians were often ambivalent about the appropriateness of emotional appeals. Edward Corbett (1971) begins his discussion of the emotional appeal on a defensive note:

People are rather sheepish about acknowledging that their opinions can be affected by their emotions. They have the uneasy feeling that there is something undignified about being stirred to action through the emotions. And, indeed, in some cases, there is something undignified about the rational man being precipitated into action through the stimulus of aroused passion. (99)

Even Aristotle, who provides a short psychology course on emotion in his *Rhetoric,* was writing in opposition to popular handbooks that overemphasized emotions, neglecting rational appeals. Emotions for Aristotle were temporary states of mind—moods—lacking the stability of reason and character.

This ambivalence about the appropriateness of emotion reflects an academic and class bias that schools seek to pass on to students. This bias, as the Dukakis fiasco suggests, is not necessarily shared by the wider culture. Students, positioned between the academic and wider culture, have to puzzle out the place of emotion and sentiment in their writing.

An informal experiment described in Cy Knoblauch and Lil Brannon (1984) provides insight into this bias. They presented a group of forty teachers with a paper that had been written by a student who had studied the events surrounding the kidnapping of the Lindbergh baby in 1927. Drawing on her research, the student had written a closing argument to the jury which the teachers were to evaluate. The argument began:

Ladies and gentlemen of the jury, I wholeheartedly believe that the evidence which has been presented before you has clearly shown that the man who is on trial here today is beyond doubt guilty of the murder of the darling, little, innocent Lindbergh baby.

Sure, the defendant has stated his innocence. But who are we to believe? Do we believe the testimony of a man who has been previously convicted; in fact, convicted of holding up innocent women wheeling baby carriages? Or do we believe the testimony of one of America's greatest heroes, Charles Lindbergh? (120)

Teachers responded to this closing argument in two ways. One group felt that the excessive emotionalism showed the writer's immaturity and lack of rhetorical skill. The other group found the piece an amusing "spoof" on the genre of trial summations.

Knoblauch and Brannon then shared with these readers excerpts from the actual summation in the case which, if anything, made greater use of the emotionalism that teachers objected to. Here is an excerpt:

Why, men and women, if that little baby, if that little curly-haired youngster, were out in the grass in the jungle, breathing, just so long as it was breathing, any tiger, any lion, the most venomous snake, would have passed that child without hurting a hair on its head. (121)

Maudlin. Sentimental. Manipulative. Purple. My own academic training has conditioned me to be on guard against this type of appeal, even to hold it in contempt. But it *was* the language of a summation that helped to convict Bruno Hauptman of murder.

The French sociologist, Pierre Bourdieu, argues that this discomfort with emotional appeals is a feature of the "aesthetic disposition" assumed by those who belong (or seek to belong) to a the cultural aristocracy (and in the United States this would include English teachers). Bourdieu (1984) made an exhaustive analysis of judgments of taste in French society and showed how these preferences have their roots in economic power, which allows a social class to distance itself from various ordinary urgencies—an attitude Bourdieu calls "bracketing." One way of bracketing, for example, is to divorce form from function—to look at a tractor, not as something to plow a field, but as an intersection of planes, ovals, and colors.

I noticed this failure to "bracket," to achieve this aesthetic distance, a few weeks ago when I visited a high school classroom where students were discussing the opening line of William Carlos Williams (1968) poem, "The Red Wheelbarrow."

So much depends
On a red wheelbarrow

A student responded, "Yeah, without the wheelbarrow, it would be hard to get things done." That interpretation had *never* occurred to me because I had disassociated (bracketed) the wheelbarrow from any function it might have. I read "depends" as referring to our need for visual vividness, the pleasure it can provide. According to Bourdieu, my "aesthetic disposition" is a form of cultural capital, a marker of social class, that we seek to pass on to students.

Another way in which bracketing works is to disassociate our aesthetic response from the conventional emotional response the content would normally elicit.

> The aesthetic disposition [tends] ... to exclude any "naïve" reaction— horror at the horrible, desire for the desirable, pious reverence for the sacred—along with all purely ethical responses, in order to concentrate solely upon the mode of representation. ... (Bourdieu 1984, 54)

The naïve reactions, these stock responses, fail to demonstrate any kind of individuating taste or discrimination. By contrast the aesthetic disposition calls for us to play with conventional evaluations of experience, to invert orders of significance. I believe "playfulness" was the quality identified by the students, quoted in Chapter 1, who spoke of the "tone of an English paper."

> She's taking something that seems menial to people and she's making a big deal. And I think they like to see stuff like that. (Newkirk 1984, 306)

The "people" in this statement may live their lives closer to what Bourdieu calls "urgencies," and may not be ready to playfully invert a sense of significance. They might find curious the academic infatuation with Virginia Woolf's "Death of a Moth" when they learn of the death of children on TV. My neighbor tells the story of taking his father, a salesman in downtown Boston, to see *Death of a Salesman* soon after it came out. Partway into the show his father turned to his son. "Who would *want* to see this?" he said and left.

In the writing classroom, a mismatch occurs if student and teacher differ in their readiness to assume a correspondence between an event and the conventional reaction to that event. A student might (reasonably) assume that a reader is predisposed to react with empathetic sadness to a story of the death of her grandmother. And in any conversational situation that might well be the reaction of the instructor. But it is likely that the instructor will treat this *written* topic with wariness, expecting something conventional, the hyphenated Death-of-the-Grandmother paper ending with a gush of sadness at the passing, yet appreciation for the wisdom the grandmother has imparted. In Chekhov's words it is a "dangerous" topic. According to the aesthetic of the instructor such papers often lack an individuating perspective. At the same time, criticism of the writing, for example a suggestion to look for some kind of originality in the scene, may seem as appropriate as laughing at a funeral.

Two Papers

In this section I examine two papers which present the issue of sentimentality in an unsettling way. The first is drawn from a cross-cultural study of evaluative standards conducted by Xiao-ming Li (1996). It is one of eight key texts she used to examine the different criteria used by Chinese and U. S. teachers in judging student writing; four texts were written by U. S. high school students and four by their counterparts in Chinese schools. Li translated each piece into the other language, and through a complex process of interviewing key readers and soliciting written evaluations, she sorted out systematic differences in evaluative criteria. She then speculated on the cultural and literary roots of these differences.

The most problematic text in the study was written by an American student. In its first draft the paper was an unfocused personal essay that dealt with parental restrictions, suicide, and nuclear war. At the suggestion of her teacher the student changed the paper into a letter to a friend who had committed suicide. I will quote the paper in full:

> The world is still going to revolve, the calendar pages are still going to turn, and life will go on as usual for most everybody. That's why it made me so mad that you committed suicide. What could you have hoped to accomplish? Yes, your problems are solved now, but ours have just begun. You've [not] only left your problems behind, but also an entire lifetime of love from family and friends and me. But you will never feel any love now, because you're dead! How could you do this to me? I'm sick and tired of taking other people's feelings into consideration! How about me? I have feelings too! You were my best friend, and now you've left me to sink or swim on my own! I am so angry and confused. Why? Why did you do that? Life would have gotten better. I know it would have.
>
> I remember the day we met like yesterday. Both of us were so alone, scared and nervous. But we met and talked. It was both of our first time at camp, so we didn't know anybody else, remember? We became immediate friends. It was the funniest week of my life. We shared our life stories, laughed and cried when the week ended. Fortunately, you lived a mere half-hour from my house. Remember all the late phone calls, telling about your first boyfriend, first kisses, your parents' divorce? I really need you now and where are you? You aren't where I need you the most, and I don't think I can forgive you for that.

Soon after we met, you told me that I was your best friend. I was so glad. I had never had a best friend before, and I felt the same about you. We told each other everything. Why was this any different?

Maybe it was me. I thought about it a lot. Maybe you tried to tell me and I wasn't listening. But you left no explanation. Just the heart-wrenching puzzle for people who cared about you to piece together.

But now, who am I to talk to, listen to? Who can I count on? Not you, because you're gone. You're gone and it hurts so much. I really need you now. I loved you like a sister. We talked to each other every night, filling hours with dreams, fantasies, and hopes. But who can I call now? I have new dreams, new hopes, ones you will never know about. There are so many things that I want to tell you but your ears will never hear me.

Of all the jumbled emotions I feel, angry, confused, and hurt, I just need you to know that I miss you. I hope that wherever you are, that you will lend an ear to listen to me. I want you to watch me grow as my anger disappears. Your life is over, at such a young age of fifteen, yet mine has just begun. I just want you to know that until we meet again, I love you, friend. (42)

As might be expected, reactions to this piece did not break evenly along national lines. Yet something curious did happen as this letter, written by a small-town New England student, was converted to the Chinese language and crossed the Pacific. *The Chinese readers liked it better than the U. S. readers.*

The U.S. readers found too much unprocessed grief in the letter. One wrote, "This unshaped, unsophisticated cry of grief belongs in a diary." Another wrote, "Uncontrolled, almost peevish. Essentially a gush." And another, "Sincerity becomes sentimentality." While a few Chinese readers shared this view, there was a more general sense of respect for the "strong, honest, sincere emotions." One of the principal readers in the study wrote this comment to the writer:

> With one after another rhetorical questions, you express to the fullest your grief for losing your best friend. There is no single word of flowery language or a false statement. This is natural beauty, genuine beauty! This is excellent! Would you like to be my friend?
>
> I wish you great success with the next piece. I believe you will succeed because you have a genuine heart. (53)

Li shows how the Chinese readers often explicitly draw from a literary tradition that has for centuries elevated poetry that expresses deep human emotion. These teachers often refer to *qing*, which has no clear English equivalent; it can mean feelings, sentiment, passion, love, or sexuality, and it can refer to the emotional appeal of a piece of writing. Li notes that the purpose of ancient

Chinese poetry was to express emotion (*qing*), to say in private what couldn't be said in public. So, paradoxically, a letter written in a small New Hampshire town had managed to find its way into the tradition of Chinese poetry.

The U. S. readers are far less explicit about literary roots for their preferences; this might be expected in a pedagogy that stresses individuality, personal voice, and the uniqueness of each writer. Yet Li argues that the tacit roots of this aesthetic lie not in poetry but in the tradition of realistic fiction. The death of the elk must be written like a police report; writers are told to "show" and not "tell." Emotion is conveyed indirectly, through implication (on the part of the writer) and inference (on the part of the reader).

The second paper I want to examine was written in my own first-year writing class. I typically have students do a considerable amount of in-class writing off some prompt (like Simic's essay in Chapter 1). Erin's paper was an extension of a piece she wrote in class about a place that for some reason mattered to her. She chose to write about a boardwalk on Cape Cod, and I'll quote the final incident she describes:

> The last time I went on the boardwalk I will never forget. It was the night before I came to UNH and my last night to see my best friend Naomi, before she went to Oxford. Naomi and I were always the closest of friends. There is no one else in the world that I can talk to like I can Naomi. The night before I left for school I picked her up and we went down to the boardwalk where we could talk. We went over to one of the jetties and just sat there for a couple of minutes, silent. The sky was full of stars and the moon was bright. The first word that was spoken was when Naomi said to me, "You are the best thing that ever came into my life. You are like another part of me and I don't think I will be able to let you go. I'm gonna miss you." We both burst into tears and we sat there hugging each other and crying for at least ten minutes. I told her how much I was going to miss her and that there was nobody else in the world that I could talk to like her, the whole time holding back my tears. I wanted to tell her everything that was on my mind, but it would have taken me forever. Sitting on the jetty reminded me of all the good times I had there in the past and now I was sitting there saying goodbye to my best friend, not knowing when I would sit there again. As we sat there crying and trying to talk between sobs, I thought about the stars and how they can be seen from all around the world. Just as if she was reading my mind Naomi looked at me and said, "Hey! If you ever start to get bummed out just remember one thing. Just look at the sky and remember we are always under the same sky." We both kind of laughed at that when we realized it sounded like something out of "The American Tail" and then we burst into tears once again. I told her we

had to go and she gave me the biggest hug ever. I told her that I loved her and she said she would miss me. I made her promise me that she would take care of herself and then I promised her the same. We both walked back to the car, holding back tears the whole way.

Another "dangerous" topic, which according to Chekhov's principle loses its effect because the language is "moistened" by more than one tear. In fact, the paper was almost literally moistened because Erin cried when she read it.

It is a paper easy to dismiss as maudlin. The language seems flat, expected, and clichéd—"I told her that I loved her and she said she would miss me," "sitting on the jetty reminded me of all the good times we had in the past," "We both walked back to the car holding back tears the whole way." There are very few individuating moments when a reader gets the sense of original or even unconventional perception or observation (the only exception being her awareness of the possible influence of "An American Tail"). In T. S. Eliot's terms, there is no "objective correlative," no formal construction that allows the reader to experience something akin to what Erin did.

Yet with only a bit of effort it is possible to play what Peter Elbow (1973) calls "the believing game" with this paper. What change in stance is required to read this as a good piece of writing? In my case, I began by watching the reaction the paper had on Erin and her classmates, who were quite moved by it when they heard her read it aloud in a response group. In order to play this believing game, it is necessary to collapse various forms of aesthetic distance, to move in closer to the paper than I normally do.

Collapse the distance between writer and audience. It was important to hear Erin read it aloud. When she did I became more aware of a gentle dignity in the language:

> I told her how much I was going to miss her
> And that there was no one else in the world
> I could talk to like her
> All the while holding back tears.

Her reading also made it harder to dismiss this experience as trite. Her presence, her actual voice, forced us all to engage in something humanly real.

Collapse the distance between reader and event. A painful parting had occurred. Something significant had happened that could not be dismissed as a cliché. And once I began to read the paper more seriously, I was struck—indeed moved—by what her friend said to her:

> You are the best thing that ever came into my life. You are another part of me and I don't think I will be able to let that go.

Her friend's outburst, suddenly breaking the silence, is a powerful statement about unconditional friendship. "The best thing that ever came into my life." How many times in our lives will any of us hear that?

Collapse the distance between ethical and aesthetic. Recall that one feature of the aesthetic stance, according to Bourdieu, is to bracket ethical concerns. By this logic we should ignore what this person says about Erin's character. Yet part of the paper's appeal is, I think, the depth of her loyalty to Naomi (indeed, Erin sent the paper to her). The closing section of the paper, stripped of moral intent, seems a cliché of parting:

> I made her promise that she would take care of herself and then I promised the same.

Yet certainly it's possible to be touched by this mutual oath.

When Mr. Wang responded to the previous paper on suicide, he wrote: "I wish you greater success with the next piece. I think you will succeed because you have a genuine heart." It's not the kind of comment a U. S. teacher is likely to make, yet the "genuine heart," the "ethic of care," shown by Erin in this piece is surely part of its appeal.

Be willing to elaborate as a reader. There is a generalized quality to the description of the parting. The jetty could be any jetty. Naomi could be any friend. The conversation is, with a couple of exceptions, only suggested. I often find that this lack of specific detail bothers me more than it bothers my students, at least early in the course (later on they realize that writing teachers *always* want more detail). I speculate that students are often readier to elaborate from their own experiences, to fill in gaps; they sometimes resist the call for a greater density of detail by saying it bogs the paper down and doesn't leave enough room for the reader's imagination. They "identify" with the writer; they "relate" to her. They seem readier than I am to bring their own experiences of saying good-bye, which in September are very fresh, to the reading of a paper like Erin's.

Be willing to endorse conventional norms of emotional response. In *The Stranger*, the main character Meursault is convicted of murder, though his real "crime" is failing to show remorse at the death of his mother. In effect, his offense is the same as Dukakis'—the inability to call up and convey an "appropriate" show of feeling. According to an aesthetic predisposition that values originality and individual distinctiveness, this conventionality seems stereotyped, unthinking, and clichéd. Meursault, though alienated and something of an antihero, does not feign emotion he does not feel.

But Erin is clearly working within traditions of sentimentalism which celebrates normative emotional reactions; this tradition is shared by the Chinese readers who do not bracket out ethical concerns (recall Mr. Wang's praise of a "good heart"). These norms endorse the expressions of connectedness, care, and self-sacrifice that point to moral and socially useful behavior. In fact, many of the qualities that we may dislike from an aesthetic perspective are the qualities of character that we would endorse in the real-life activity of our students. The lack of ambivalence and complexity might be seen, from another standpoint, as the unconditional and wholehearted commitment of the writer.

To put the issue in more literary terms, there are certain tropes, or conventional resonating images, that the implied reader in this piece is open to. The primary and most obvious conventional image is that of tears, which establish the depth of emotion and sympathy of the two friends. The other primary image is that of the setting—alone, outside on a clear night, near enough to the ocean to hear the sound of the waves. The presence of the natural world serves as a balm to the pain of the parting. Technically, I suppose, this parting could have occurred in a bar after several beers, yet the effect would be entirely different, away from the consoling powers of sea and sky.

My intention in this chapter is not to argue that we should treat all sincere expressions of emotion as good writing, but to understand the roots of the often reflexive rejection of pieces like Erin's. In other words, it is important for teachers of composition to explicitly locate reading responses within literary traditions (as the Chinese teachers in Li's study did). To do so requires a brief excursion into the debate about "sentimentality" in American literature and the way that term has been used to dismiss the writing of women—including arguably the most significant novel written in this country, *Uncle Tom's Cabin*.

According to Nina Baym, the critics who helped establish the canon of the great American male writer relied on the criterion, not of literary merit (whatever that might be), but of "Americaness." The cultural myth at the root of "Americaness" was essentially a male version of self-actualization:

> The myth narrates a confrontation of the American individual, the pure American self divorced from specific social circumstances, with the promise offered by the idea of America. This promise is the deeply romantic one that in the new land, untrammelled by history and social accident, a person will be able to achieve complete self-definition. (1985, 71)

According to this standard, domestic literature, which focuses on a specific setting and a web of social and moral responsibilities (including friendship), would be less American, less "great." Even in Erin's piece there is no single protagonist, no individuated point of view, one in which she differentiates herself from the perspective of her friend. We are to imagine that their feelings are essentially alike.

The modernist criteria of emotional displacement provided (and continues to provide) a justification for dismissing sentimental literature. T. S. Eliot claimed the artist does not communicate in the more direct way of a Stowe or Dickens; instead the author disappears, transforming emotion into formal structures, which are the "objective correlatives" of the emotional sense the author seeks to convey. The tenets of this modernism were translated into Strunk and White's injunction to use "specific concrete language"; we get similar advise from George Orwell when he suggests that words be "windows," open to some outer reality. In its simplest form it is the regular incantation to "show" and not "tell." Direct expressions of emotion spoil the inferential pleasure of reading. According to this standard, Erin's piece does not show enough. By communicating feeling directly, writer to audience, it does not give the reader enough inferential space.

I suspect that for most readers in my generation, the impact of this aesthetic came when we first read Hemingway's short stories, the shocking emotional scarceness of "Hills Like White Elephants" or "The Killers." In one of his stories, "Soldier's Home," there is a direct confrontation between a typical Hemingway protagonist and the sentimental discourse Hemingway sought to undermine.

In the story Harold Krebs, who had fought in some of the major battles of World War I, returns home and finds himself alienated from his hometown, his family, and even from himself as he begins to "lie" about his war service. He begins to look back to his wartime service as a time of personal purity:

> A distaste for everything that had happened to him in the war set in because of the lies he told. All of the times that had been able to make him feel cool and clear inside himself when he thought of them; the times so long back when he had done the one thing, the only thing for a man to do, easily and naturally, when he might have done something else, now lost their cool, valuable quality, and then were lost themselves. (1938, 145–46)

His aimlessness worries his parents, and in the climactic scene his mother confronts the issue. When she finishes her exhortation, Krebs replies coolly, "Is that all?"

> "Yes. Don't you love your mother, dear boy?"
> "No," Krebs said.

His mother looked at him across the table. Her eyes were shiny. She started crying.

Krebs realizes he has hurt her badly and says, not very convincingly, that he didn't really mean it. The tension seems to ease.

Krebs kissed her hair. She put her face to him.
"I'm your mother," she said. "I held you next to my heart when you were a tiny baby."
Krebs felt sick and vaguely nauseated. (152)

Here are the emblems of sentimentality—tears, an infant held to a mother's heart—turned into a smothering form of dishonesty. They force Krebs into new deceptions, into conventional expressions of filial love, which, lie-by-lie, take him away from that "cool valuable quality" he had experienced as a soldier. For the story to "work" our sympathies need to be primarily with Krebs, who is still longing for some uncomplicated, undomesticated sense of who he is.

The story is also an aesthetic lesson. Like Krebs (Hemingway implies), we are threatened by conventional expressions of emotion ("I held you next to my heart when you were a tiny baby"). Such expressions interfere with any possibility of self-awareness or emotional integrity; Krebs has no legitimate way of answering his mother's question about whether he loves her. He is caught in the web of conventionality, trapped by conventional maternal affection.

I wonder if our instinctive reaction when reading papers like Erin's mirrors that of Krebs. We have been taught to be "vaguely nauseated" by the emblems of sentimentality that presuppose a corresponding emotional reaction on our part. It is part of our aesthetic mythology that values what Krebs values—that sense of particularity that made him feel "cool and clear inside himself." But to give in to this nausea also entails distancing ourselves from the ways emotion is expressed and expected in the wider culture that some students draw on. Reading against the grain can help us step outside our own aesthetic and appreciate papers which assume different and more direct conventions for emotional expression.

4

Reach for the Stars

Don't wait to be a great man. Be a great boy.
—Sign in the Ashland, Ohio, YMCA, 1959

Alan, a former wrestler, was a student in my Freshman English class several years ago. He came from a family of wrestlers; his brother, whom he idolized, had been the state champion in Maine. Alan wrote his first paper of the course on his brother, and I learned about the systematic way this brother prepared for the wrestling season—diet, weight lifting, roadwork. I learned that this dedication to sports did not interfere with schoolwork. I learned that in what little spare time the brother had he worked as a Big Buddy to an elementary school child and donated his time to sports clinics. His brother seemed perfect, if one-dimensional.

In the conference with Alan I probed, diplomatically I thought, ways in which he might make this profile more complex. Did his brother have a humorous side? What gave him difficulty? Was there, perhaps, a negative sound to this single-mindedness? As I recall, Alan nodded his head at my questions, but made no revisions and chose not to include the paper in the group he handed in for a grade. On the course evaluation he wrote, "Mr. Newkirk is a pretty good teacher, but for some reason he doesn't like my brother."

Alan and I were miscommunicating about more than writing. This exchange concerned the nature of heros, the difference between conditional and unconditional admiration; we were talking across an ideological divide and not incidentally an age divide. In this chapter I look at the mismatch in worldviews that occurs when students present themselves in personal writing. I particularly want to look at student optimism as an irritant; the way this optimism can easily be perceived as shallow, naïve, unsophisticated. Papers like Alan's and others in this chapter are frequently sites of a developmental clash.

In classic depictions of human development, this clash is often seen as a given. Here, for example, is an excerpt from Aristotle's depiction of the youthful temperament:

> And they are not cynical, but guileless, because of not yet having seen much wickedness. And they are trusting, because of not yet having been much

deceived. And they are filled with good hopes; for like those drinking wine, the young are heated by their nature, and at the same time they are filled with hopes because of not having experienced much failure. And they live for the most part in hope for the future, and memory is of what has gone by, but for the young the future is long and the past is short. . . . ([338 BCE] 1991, 165)

Samuel Johnson ([1752] 1969) echoes Aristotle, "Hope will predominate in every mind till it has been suppressed by frequent disappointments." A corollary of this belief is a heightened sense of agency, the belief that future success and happiness is almost solely dependent on the will and effort of the individual:

> He is inclined to believe no man miserable but by his own fault, and seldom looks with much pity upon failings and miscarriages because he thinks them willingly admitted and negligently incurred. (258)

Johnson touches on the problem of response when he notes that it is "impossible" to hear young people talk of future plans and expectations without feeling some pity and contempt.

It is tempting to dismiss these conventional descriptions as archaic and unrelated to the situations of our students today. But in surveys of college students, one thing that stands out is their personal optimism. In a survey reported by David Levine, President of Teachers College, Columbia, students were generally pessimistic about the country's social institutions—the media, government, corporations, even the American family. Yet a robust majority, nine out of every ten respondents, were optimistic about their personal futures.

This optimism may interfere with the performance of self expected in the personal essay. According to Phillip Lopate (1994), the personal essay frequently gives a "middle aged point of view":

> [The personal essay] is the fruit of ripened experience, which naturally brings with it some worldly disenchantment, or at least realism. With middle age comes a taste for equilibrium; hence, that stubborn, almost unnerving calm that so often pervades the essay. (xxxvi)

Models presented to students in anthologies—E. B. White's "Once More to the Lake," "Shooting an Elephant," Edward Hoagland's "The Courage of Turtles"—all reflect this mature viewpoint. Lopate argues that for developmental reasons these models are difficult for young writers to emulate:

> A young person still thinks it is possible—there is time enough—to become all things. . . . Later, knowing one's fate and accepting the responsibility of

that uninnocent knowledge define the perspective of the [personal essay] form. (xxxvii)

It does not follow from Lopate's analysis that young writers should not be invited to write personal essays, or, as some critics of personal writing maintain, that students "have nothing to really say about their lives" because they lack critical distance. The desire to make sense of what we see and do does not suddenly come upon us in midlife. I have always believed that students appreciate the chance to write about their lives and interests—and the regular opportunity to read these accounts has literally kept me teaching composition.

Happy Endings

We can begin with endings. The essay differs from the narrative in that we expect a reflective turn, when the writer stands back from the specific information and generalizes about it. These turns, which are the subject of Chapter 2, answer the "so what" question. They can happen throughout the essay, but the ending is an obvious spot for summing up, and it is often a spot where the experienced reader feels let down in student essays. Let's look at two examples.

"Life's Lessons from Childhood Cancer" was written as a college admission essay in response to the common prompt to "write about a significant experience in your life." The writer, Moriah McGrath, was diagnosed with cancer of the kidney when she was four and had to undergo a painful regime of chemotherapy:

> Cancer is a frightening disease, and it is difficult for a child to deal with it. I can still remember feeling uncomfortable in the hospital's spooky corridors. I will also never forget the way I kicked and screamed when the doctors and nurses tried to administer chemotherapy. I made such a fuss because I knew how the chemicals felt as they ran up the veins in my arm, and I knew how sick I would be later. . . .

The memories were not all painful: she recalls the Easter when the tubes were taken out of her nose and she was wheeled around the hospital, collecting seven baskets filled with candy.

She concludes by looking at what this experience has done for her. Here are the final two paragraphs:

> Although I have absolutely no desire to go through it again, having cancer did have positive effects on my life. I grew up knowing that cancer can be a fatal disease, so I always have hope for people who fall ill. I always think that anyone can get better because I was blessed with such good luck. Having

cancer also taught me that I was a strong person. I may have shed many a tear along the way, but I did make it through all my treatments.

Even more remarkable is the fact that I went to school with no hair on my head feeling completely self-confident. If I endured cancer when I was four, I'm sure I'll be able to handle anything life dishes out. (*Boston Globe*, January 14, 1995)

In this essay, adversity is treated as a challenge that, once surmounted, makes the writer a stronger, better person. Her own sense of empowerment—the fact she has recovered—gives her hope both that others can do the same and that she herself can handle any other obstacles in her way. As I read this ending an adult voice in my head said, "Nobody can handle anything life dishes out." The very fact that she admits to being "lucky" suggests that. Yet to question her conclusion (in the name of "good writing" of course) would be to challenge this writer's sense of her own power. Is it our job to "problematize" this belief?

The conventional descriptions of "youth" overlook the trauma that is so visible in student writing (even Samuel Johnson lived an excruciating childhood). The single most persistent, painful, and debilitating experience I read about concerns the effects of divorce. At one group meeting in my office a student read his paper about the vicious tug-of-war between his divorced parents. When he finished a student in the group nodded, "I know what you mean." Then everyone else nodded.

I asked, "You mean you're all from divorced families?"

They nodded again.

The sense of betrayal and desertion (by the father, usually) is often raw. Here is an account by Nicole Lavesque of the morning her father broke the news of the separation:

Later in the morning he took us to breakfast. It was a very uncomfortable meal that lasted a long time. I don't recall much of the conversation but I know I had a giant lump in my throat the whole time and I think my dad did too. He gave us a speech about how it was not our faults that they were separating, it was between him and my mom. We just did not understand, that there was no way it was just between them, of course it had something to do with my sister and me. We were involved whether he liked it or not. He went on to answer my sister's question of "why?" and his answer floored us. He told us he didn't love her anymore. This was a slap in the face to both of us because none of this had been apparent to us. It was almost as if we had landed on another planet, that looked exactly like ours, and this was someone else's miserable life we accidently got involved in.

Nicole finishes her essay on a half note, as if while the pain has receded the recollection of what happened constitutes a dangerous memory:

> The separation is not something we think about on a daily basis anymore, but it will always be in the back of our minds and surely has changed who we are today.

Other students work to make the memory less dangerous by working the incident into a larger narrative of their own self-development. For without this master scheme, the events remain painfully raw and uninstructive. They resist viewing their childhood trauma as permanently disabling; better to see it as a lesson that makes them stronger or more independent. From the standpoint of the writing, though, these resolutions may seem clichéd, even a retreat from the difficult emotional issues raised in the piece.

This tension can be illustrated by Marissa Serge's paper on the divorce that devastated the childhood of one of her friends. In it, Marissa shows how Julia has "been through hell and back with this divorce." Here is one incident:

> I remember one tension filled experience between her parents that still eats at Julia to this day. We were freshmen in high school and our parents came to see us play a district soccer game. Julia had the game of her life. We were both flying with happiness at the end of the game when we went to talk to both sets of parents [both had remarried], who were oddly enough, standing next to each other. As we both bounced up to them we could feel the tension in the air. Her mother half-heartedly grumbled a "hello girls" as her father shot a "lets get out of here now" glance. As Julia followed her father, she looked back at me with tear filled eyes. I will never forget her look of disappointment and sadness. Her success was completely shattered by her parents unwillingness to even try to get along.

After relating several incidents like this one, Marissa notes that Julia, understandably, has an extremely hard time trusting other people; her relationship with her boyfriend is strained for fear she will end up like her parents. She concludes her next-to-last paragraph, "This experience has been destructive to who she is as a person."

Marissa chooses, however, not to end the paper on that note. She concludes as follows:

> Although this experience has been very damaging, I think it made Julia a stronger, more independent person. I admire these qualities in her. She

turned this situation to her advantage in the one way that she could; by making her a better person.

This conclusion seems to come out of the blue, clashing sharply with the sentence that came before. The divorce has been "destructive" to Julia as a person—yet because of it she is a better person. When I spoke to Marissa in conference I pointed out how this last paragraph doesn't seem to fit the paper, which shows the destructive power of divorce; we get nothing remotely comparable showing the stronger, more resilient Julia. I suggested that since the point of the paper seemed to be to show the damage divorce causes that she should consider rewriting or eliminating the final paragraph. Marissa chose to keep it.

I now see how this final paragraph fits Julia's experience into a narrative of self-development. She rises from the destruction of the previous paragraph: this parental indifference actually enables her to become an independent person able to deal with adversity. This is the plot of virtually every young adult novel—unreliable or absent parents create a space for the self-development of the protagonist. There is a redemptive reward to the pain and parental indifference. By refusing to eliminate the last paragraph, Marissa provides a scheme that transforms hardship into an opportunity for growth and allows her to see her friend as strengthened and not destroyed.

This is the alchemy of optimism, the ability to transform the disagreeable. It is the central themes of Joseph Conrad's ([1903] 1966) haunting story of optimism, "Youth." In it Marlowe recounts his first voyage, a comedy of mishaps, leaks, the ship catching on fire, abandoning ship—all transformed by the young Marlowe into something joyful. As the lifeboats set out from the sinking ship, we get the same abrupt transformation of negative to positive, the same alchemy, that was evident in Marissa's paper:

> I remember sixteen hours on end with a mouth dry as a cinder and a steering oar over the stern to keep my first command head on to a breaking sea. I did not know how good a man I was till then. I remember the drawn faces, the dejected figures of my two men, and I remember my youth and the feeling that will never come back any more—the feeling that I can last forever, outlast the sea, the earth, all men; the deceitful feeling that lures us to joys, to perils, to love, to vain effort—to death; the triumphant conviction of strength, the heat of life in the handful of dust, the glow in the heat that with every year grows dim, grows cold, grows small, and expires—and expires, too soon, too soon—before life itself. (202–203)

Ah, youth.

The Right to Believe

A couple of years ago a Reubens exhibit came to the Boston Museum of Fine Arts. Local newspapers and magazines were filled with reproductions, often juxtaposed, unintentionally, with current advertisements for jeans, some featuring the superthin model Kate Moss. It seemed to me a good lesson for my Freshman English class on how culture and media can construct completely different images of female beauty. To say the lesson was a bomb would be inaccurate; it was more like one of the rockets Wily Coyote sends out that turns and comes after him.

As I recall, most of the conversation centered around the Kate Moss picture. Wasn't there some danger, I asked, in this almost anorectic image being presented to young women? Isn't it an impossible, even unhealthy ideal? The women in the class sensed no danger at all. One commented that this was only one way of looking attractive, not the only way. Another said that the jean ads actually expanded the range of attractive images; she liked the fact that Moss's body type could be considered attractive. In a sense, it was one more new look. Choices had been enhanced. So a lesson in social construction turned 180 degrees and became a lesson in students' virtually unlimited belief in their own power to choose.

In composition theory today, this orientation with its exalted sense of individual agency is often treated as the base position from which a more sophisticated sense of self and culture needs to be constructed. The student possesses what the existentialists would call "false consciousness" because they uncritically accept various cultural myths embodied in commonplaces —"life is what you make it," "winners never quit and quitters never win." Because these myths stress *individual* agency they prepare the student for the role of individual consumer and minimize the role of collective action that is needed for real political change. The student, in this base position, is co-opted, mired in dualistic thinking, naïve, still at that entry level of awareness. There is often a convert-the-natives attitude in these descriptions of students, without a corresponding attempt to understand the belief systems that are being supplanted.

Those who champion "academic discourse" often similarly dismiss these commonplaces as entirely outside the kind of conversations students are to engage in. This folk wisdom is, in fact, the "other" that academicians define themselves against; it embodies given cultural assumptions that must be "problematized." The clearest example is the widely influential description of the University of Pittsburgh basic writing course in David Bartholomae and Anthony Petrosky's *Facts, Artifacts, and Counterfacts* (1986). One of the first assignments in the course is to describe a significant experience and explain its significance. Here is one response to the assignment that the authors find problematic:

> When I went to South Catholic I became friends with my spanish teacher, his name was Brother Larwarance Dempsey. He was a great teacher and also assistant Coach to the wrestling team. One day he invited me down to the weight-training room, he showed me a few of the machines and how to use them. Since he was just starting to lift weights I wanted to start to. That October he wanted me to go out for the wrestling team. I was scared to death a little pudgy kid like me.
>
> He had such spirit and drive that I stuck with it. He always boaste me by saying "fire up." I really got into weights after the season and running. I became more confident. As fast as it went the next year came I was down a weight class and ready to go I beat 5 kids for the position and went first string varsity the rest of my junior year. At the end of the year we all got word that brother Larry was going to Jersey City. I was very disappointed because I know I'd miss him. I was losing my confidence and almost gave up the sport. I then had to decide what to do. I was determined now more than before but this time make it on my own the next year I became team Captian.
>
> If you work hard and follow the rules things will get better and better. (33–34)

The authors refer dismissively to this essay as a "*Boy's Life* narrative"; the student, they argue, falls back on the authoritative language of parents, coaches, and other powerful adults. He does not yet possess the "remarkable muscularity of mind" needed to push against this given discourse.

> To the student who wrote the paper above, we can only say, "No, that's not it," and then do what we can to characterize what it is that he has done that we can't accept. (34)

There are, of course, options other than saying, "that's not it." We can listen to the story. We could express admiration for the way the writer transformed himself from an overweight kid to the team captain. That is an impressive achievement. We could also show curiosity by asking him to fill in some of the gaps in the story—how he was able to carry on without his mentor present. Finally we might ask ourselves what motive (other than pleasing us) this writer has for "problematizing" a code of belief that has served him so well. It seems a peculiar form of bait-and-switch to ask students to write about the significance in their lives and then to recoil when they speak of the virtues of hard work and perseverance.

On the principle that we should not set out to change what we don't understand, I would like to make the case for the *empowerment* that comes from cultural commonplaces stressing personal agency. I'll begin by accepting the constructionist belief that the "autonomous self" that makes "individual decisions" is a cultural myth; in fact, if we look carefully, or even casually, it is evident that our choices are constrained by our position in families, communities, language systems, political units—the list goes on.

A pragmatist like William James would begin by saying yes, I suppose these can be seen as myths, and "personal freedom to choose" may be one more cultural construction. But he would go on to ask what the "cash value," the "utility" of this belief is. To argue that skepticism and critique are the most valid intellectual positions is reminiscent of the claim that James opposed in which scientific certainty was the only form of truth worth acting on. James would claim that cultural criticism and scientific positivism both do a poor job of creating space for belief; in Peter Elbow's terms they favor the "doubting game" over the "believing game" (1973). The value of a belief like that of personal agency ("life is what you make it") cannot be discredited on the basis of cultural critique by claiming to show its "constructedness" or by challenging the "essentialism" of the claim for a "self." The pragmatist would look to the consequences of the belief.

For James, the act of believing is necessary for the verification of the belief itself. Suppose I need to jump a big ditch and my ability to do this is in doubt—yet I believe that I can; that belief is a crucial component of the experiment I am attempting. Without it I cannot make a true test of my ability; or as James ([1896], 1948) writes, "The desire for a certain form of truth here brings about the special truth's existence." He continues:

> Who gains promotions, boons, appointments, but the man in whose life they are seen to play the part of live hypothesis . . . who sacrifices other things for their sake before they have come, and takes risks for them in advance? His faith acts on the powers above him as a claim, and creates its own verification. (104)

Faith in a fact, he states, can help create the fact. An unconditional belief in one's agency, James might argue, can be empowering, can carry its own verification. Those who believe they are responsible for acting morally are more likely to act morally than those who see themselves as victims of social forces. And a wholehearted belief may have more "cash value" than a thoroughly problematized one.

In this light the "commonplaces" so easily dismissed in works like *Facts, Artifacts, and Counterfacts* might be seen instead as empowering, self-verifying myths. The student that writes about the value of "never giving up" may not simply be mouthing a cliché passed on from authoritative adults, but expressing his belief in a code of conduct that has paid off handsomely, a belief become fact. My point is not that we should simply endorse the uncritical acceptance of the commonplaces; only that we recognize their value and not turn them into intellectual indiscretions.

I suspect that if I look at my own value system honestly, particularly when it is put to some test, I endorse many of the same values embodied in these commonplaces, and use the same language. As Laurie Quinn (1996) has written:

> When terrible things happen, many of us—including writing teachers—reach for expressions that serve as makeshift suture kits for the resulting wounds. The words are never adequate but we say them and sometimes write them anyway; they are familiar and comforting in their familiarity. . . . They are meant to dissolve barriers, serve as common ways of phrasing our shared perceptions and emotions. They close the gap between people, to make the pain of life seem less isolating.

A few weeks ago I learned that a friend of mine has been diagnosed with a reoccurrence of cancer, and the prognosis was dreadful. I knew I should phone her—wanted to phone her—but I was almost incapacitated because I didn't know what to say. Finally I made the call, and like many brave cancer patients she made it easy for me. I ended the call by saying I wanted to see her soon, and that she should "hang in there." At this margin of life and death, I had reached a spot where the only words that could work for me were the well-used commonplaces of concern and motivation.

It is hardly surprising that students draw on the literature of self-direction. It is the language of the exhortation, the language of encouragement, an antidote to insecurity, indecision, and the lack of confidence. It is everywhere—on the *New York Times* best-seller list, the locker-room slogans, the quiet, late-night conversations of friends. Many openly attribute their success as students and athletes to the convincing use of this form of exhortation—and they must surely be puzzled when they find this discourse of resoluteness challenged by teachers as lacking complexity, as romantic, and, most disparaging of all, as naïve.

The Pastoral

Romanticism offers other resources for optimism to the young writer. Just as coaches, teachers, and parents can activate and promote a vigorous sense of personal agency, the natural world itself can be seen as a counselor. One of the major tendencies in romantic evocations of nature is, what Lawrence Buell (1995) has termed, "nature's personhood." Buell quotes a letter of George Perkin March to illustrate this tendency:

> In those juvenile days, the bubbling brook, the trees, the wild animals were to me persons, not things, and though not of a poetical nature, I sympathized with those *beings,* as I have never done since with the *general* society of men. (180)

In student writing, the natural world, if attended to, can help the writer/ observer reestablish a sense of equanimity by clarifying goals, by separating the secondary from the primary. The writing is structured as a progression from a state of anxiety or indecision to one of renewed focus.

We can see this pattern in a paper chosen by the late Roger Garrison for the collection *What Makes Writing Good* (Coles and Vopat 1985). The writer, Karen Tocher, begins in a state of psychological disarray:

> Last night, deep inside me, a storm was brewing—and I exploded. Oh, the tears, the anger, and the overwhelming sense of sadness and loneliness. The wine I drank—too much—was just fuel for the fire. (270)

Almost immediately, with the suggestion of an internal "storm," there is a blurring of boundaries between the natural nonhuman realm and inner psychological states. She continues the pastoral theme as she decides to take a bike ride:

> I dug my bicycle out of the cluttered barn and pedaled in the winter afternoon sunshine. How simple that bike is, no pouring of gas to make a big greasy engine run. (270)

She comes to a field where the "gurgle of a brook along the roadside stopped my pedaling." It is as if nature itself is taking control, stopping her from going on—as if this is a planned encounter that leads to the central moment of instruction.

> The field was bordered by huge pine and birch trees, and an old stone wall. In the middle of the field, a bare apple tree stood alone. Its stark branches seemed to reach out to me. I put my bike down and walked into the field. The snow crunched and the soles of my sneakers imprinted a trail of tiny stars. When I finally reached the apple tree, I stretched out on my back and looked up into the blue gleaming sky. A dozen white sea gulls dived and soared in the crystal air. Far in the distance I heard some crows. They reminded me of the little people I cared for at the day care center. "B for

ball, C for crow. What does a crow say? Let me hear you!" and the children shout "CAAAAWWWW!" with big smiles on their faces. (270)

Soon her thoughts were "as clear as the air." The encounter, the lesson, was orchestrated by the natural world: the brook has stopped her, the tree has beckoned her, and the birds had taught her, renewing her vocational focus.

According to Buell, this tendency toward personification has often been embarrassing to American modernist writers. Wallace Stevens (1973, "Delightful Evening") consistently showed his disgust at the very metaphor used by Tocher:

> The spruce's outstretched hands;
> The twilight overfull
> Of wormy metaphors.

Xiao-ming Li's (1996) study suggests that, at least among Chinese writing teachers, there may be a greater receptiveness to this romantic evocation of nature. One of the prize-winning compositions she includes follows almost exactly the pattern Karen Tocher used. The piece is titled, "Me, Before and After the Exam." The writer has been nominated to represent his class in a composition contest—on the same day he is to take an ornithology test. This situation depresses him, as he knows he will deeply disappoint one of his teachers.

His moment of illumination came as he watched the sunset:

> Looking up, I watched the clouds gradually disappearing around the edge of the sky. Yet the setting sun was still so charming, red as blood, as fire, more beautiful in her final glow. A flock of wild birds flew in front of her, and a minute later, a flock of doves, flapping their joyful wings, flew toward her. What a beautiful sunset! Yes, that beauty belonged to Mother Nature. Loving the birds, taking care of the birds, was what my heart desired. I said to myself, "Love the birds and do something for the birds. That is what you can give to Nature." I looked up at the setting sun again; happy ducks were charging toward the sun and flying away. I must conquer myself for those happy birds, for the magnificent beauty of the nature before me! (23)

The Chinese evaluator of this essay identified "the repeated brilliant descriptions of the setting sun" as the essay's great strength, though the American readers found it overdramatic and sentimental.

According to Buell (1995), one "ingredient" of an environmental text is the conviction that "the nonhuman environment is present not merely as a framing device but as a presence that begins to suggest that human history is implicated in natural history" (7). This "implication" often takes the form of describing parallel processes in the human and nonhuman spheres. Human aging parallels the changing seasons; sunrises evoke optimistic beginnings; clouds represent doubt or depression—the list easily expands, so automatic is this form of association. Yet trivial and clichéd as it often seems, this "implication" can be profoundly stabilizing and ennobling as humans try to extend the capacity to identify beyond the human sphere. In the next paper, the writer draws on this literary convention.

"My Place" is a description of a farm and the devout older couple who ran it. Almost immediately the human and nonhuman are blurred:

> As much as the farm stands out in my mind, the people who owned it do so even more for Mr. and Mrs. Knowles were unique. What made them content was their love of life. They had no goal like most of us need. They searched for no purpose like most of us do. Instead they spent their days thanking God for giving them life. *They were like a mother and father to everything and everyone.* (emphasis added)

Even inanimate matter is vivified, parented.

In an eloqent last paragraph, the writer, Jim Emond, returns to the farm long after it had been burned to the ground:

> Today as I write this I look around and see not too much has changed with this place. The land has been leveled where the house and barn used to be. The chicken coop and sugar shack still remain, the first packed with cord wood, the latter a home for a number of squirrels. The tracter tire is still hanging from the weather beaten rope, forever oscillating in the breeze. But most important, the simplicity and tranquility of yesterday remain. The land seems to have inherited it from the people who once lived there.

Here the metaphor of mutuality is continued; where earlier the couple acted as mother and father, we see their inheritance of simplicity and goodness passed on to the land itself. This vision is for the writer, a representation of an unalienated existence.

Another way to suggest this mutuality is to explore seasonal changes, a basic strategy of classic environmental texts such as *Walden* and *Sand County Almanac*. At one level the reoccurrence of the seasons involves us in cyclical time, as opposed to the progressive process of aging. It is to be in touch with something reassuringly *permanent*. Andrea Rollins opens her paper, "Sapping," by evoking a point in seasonal change between winter and spring:

> There is a time between winter and spring. It usually comes in late February or early March when winter seems tired and spring is only hoped for. The whiteness of January has disappeared and there is no resemblance of

spring in the air. It is the time when the nights are dreadfully cold with the March winds whipping through the trees and the days turn into melting sunshine.

The paper describes the process of tapping maple trees and making syrup, a tradition that goes back one hundred years in her family. The season ends with a sapping party where the syrup is boiled thick as caramel, and dribbled in the last patches of snow to harden. She ends her paper by evoking her original image of seasonal change:

> The sugaring off party means the sapping has come to end. Throughout the summer the trees grow leafier and greener because of the sap that begins circulating under the bark and nourishing the tree in March. It is almost sad to pack away the all the buckets and covers until next year, but it is comforting to know that deep in the roots and just under the bark, the green trees are quietly making sap and storing it for that time of year, when winter seems tired and spring is only hoped for.

The trees themselves seem to consciously cooperate, making and storing sap for this time of year. They also seem humanized by her description of the sap "circulating" through the roots under the bark.

Buell notes that even environmental writers have often been embarrassed by this tendency to personify nature. Yet the persistence of the trope of "nature's personhood" suggests it plays a role in cultivating a sense of accountability for the environment. Once trees are perceived as Andrea perceives them, as partners in the process of sapping, as virtual bodies with sap circulating under an epidermis—it becomes harder to acquiesce in their destruction. We see this ethical turn in Karen Tocher's paper. After seeing the birds, and being reminded of her pleasure in working with children, she reflects on these farms:

> Many of the farms are deteriorating, but their owners hold onto the land. They are too proud to sell to greedy developers, who will scar the land with suburban sprawl. I fear the death of the old farmers; for then the land where I lay in solitude today will have side-by-side houses, driveway loops, and an asphalt playground. The apple tree will either get chopped down to make room for a garage, or the neighbors will fight over the crabbed fruit. (Coles and Vopat 1985)

She has no specific way to prevent this future, but the urge to resist environmental degradation arises from our own imaginative capacity to see our own lives as coextensive with the natural world.

If, as I have argued, students entering college have a psychological need to view their lives as progressive narratives, it is not difficult to see why they are drawn to the two romantic traditions I have briefly identified. The literature of self-direction suggests that this future is claimable if there is sufficient personal will. It protects against fatalism, helplessness, and determinism. It transforms that which is disagreeable and painful into stategically placed obstacles that both teach and strengthen. This possibility of progress and self-actualization is enhanced if the student has access to mentors to guide the process. In the next chapter I will examine the role of teachers and older adults. But drawing from a tradition of American romanticism—nature writing—students can also depict the nonhuman environment as a consoling and clarifying counselor.

The Gentle Counterpressure

Still, these commonplaces, appearing in written essays unanalyzed and simply invoked, can cause us to feel, "No, that's not it." The following paper is an example. The author, Jon Wilson, was a graduate of a Catholic high school where much of what he wrote was "brief and to the point." At the beginning of his Freshman English course he is writing "brief-and-to-the-point sentences" where his teacher is pushing him to bring more out of his topic. "More Sports!" is a revision of an autobiographical paper written in the first couple weeks of the course. It begins:

> Have you ever been a part of a sports team and realized that you are part of something, that is more than just playing games, that acts or represents a model of a disciplined way of life. If you thought the last sentence did not make sense then you are a spectator. In the following paper I have shown my career in sports is one example of redefining myself or developing myself. The use of redefine is not exaggerating because sports has changed my life in all aspects and I think that I would be a totally different person if I had not been involved in sports. It was during high school that most of my involvement in sports took place.

The paper then begins a chronology of his sports career—his early success, his extensive work with weights, making the varsity team in his sophomore year. In that year he also played junior varsity football, which was much looser and more enjoyable:

> Just before a junior varsity game everybody was very loud. We listened to loud music and our coaches drove about 80 miles per hour on the way to the game. We were always whistling at girls in cars that flew by and we were

just plain obnoxious. We were also very confident in ourselves. During the football games we would slaughter the other team. During this time period my coaches gave very little guidance on respect for the other team, but gave us plenty of guidance of how to respect ourselves. . . . After the game we would scream, yell, and make really big messes at McDonald's. We were rowdy and we were very close. I believe that's why we were so successful.

In his junior year he transferred to a bigger public high school, and the training became more serious. He and his teammates were successful because they had learned some very important "life lessons": "We learned discipline and a work ethic." The attitude carried over into his senior year when he won the state championship in both the discus and shotput. Jon concludes:

I have had a very successful four years in high school athletics. What came out of all this is a person that is organized, disciplined, and devoted. I hope that I can improve myself everyday by learning more and more so that one day I can get a Ph.D. in Computer Science. I have joined the ROTC at the university so I can achieve my goals. I will always be a part of something whether it be a classroom, research development team, or a sports team.

This is an easy paper to dislike, a classic example of what is not so affectionately called the "male jock" paper among our staff. It seems a string of under-elaborated episodes all showing the same thing—the value of discipline and hard work. Yet I don't think the most useful response is to say, "This isn't it."

To play Elbow's believing game, we first need to listen for the intended message. Jon has, through extraordinarily hard work, become a successful football player and one of the state's outstanding track and field athletes. He has reached a level of excellence only a tiny fraction of athletes ever reach. It seems reasonable to acknowledge this achievement and to recognize that he attributes his success to a work ethic that he is probably not going to throw into serious question.

Which doesn't mean that the writing teacher cannot exert a gentle counterpressure, even working within the student's ideology. The key word "discipline" seems saturated with meanings; it operates as a code word that defines every phase of his development. Yet there are suggestions that his use of the term changes. At the end of the paper he seems to exercise more thorough self-control than he did on the junior varsity football team when he and his buddies were trashing McDonald's.

Jon's teacher takes a somewhat different route to the same goal by asking him, "What is the paper about?":

Jon: Life lessons.

Gene: What about them?

Jon: Through (*pause*)—What about them? That's a pretty good question. What about them? Life lessons. Maybe "life lessons" is too general. Um, maybe the discipline that it took me to get to where I am right now.

Gene: OK. Maybe one life lesson.

Then Jon provides a long turn in which he begins to look more deeply into his key term:

Jon: Yeah, but I mention other things about you know things that were brought about in me like if it wasn't for football I don't think I would have joined student government and I was able to get up in front of two hundred people and stand up there for five minutes and speak about why they should elect me to be their senate member and I was . . . I did very well and I wasn't nervous and I don't know . . . football just gave me confidence and I'm not saying the sport itself gave me confidence. But what I had to do to be good at the sport, the things I had to face up to, the challenges.

When I went to practice I had to like compete with other teammates who were my friends and the next day in school . . . you know you have to speak with these people every day. They're your friends. You interact with them and at the same time you're competing. You're trying to win and at the same time you're mature enough not to say, "Oh, I made the varsity."

Gene then scaffolds Jon's comments by providing a conceptual frame ("two elements") he might consider:

Gene: OK, so it sounds like you're talking about at least two different elements of why football is important to you.

Jon: What are the two different elements?

Gene: The two I'm hearing is the first one is that it affected you academically or at least it gave you confidence. Um, the second is you talking about your interaction with your teammates. So how are those two bound?

Jon: The interaction with teammates is just something that comes with football. I mean you have to interact. I think the main theme of the paper is discipline and it took me discipline to interact I guess in a mature fashion.

In this exchange Jon seems to work toward a concept of discipline ("discipline to interact") that is distinct from discipline that allows him to meet challenges (giving the speech), and discipline that enables him to build physical strength.

Although this conference did not produce a reconceptualized paper or even a substantially revised one, I believe that Gene has worked within what Lad Tobin (1993) calls a zone of "productive tension"—pushing for clarification and analysis without challenging the value system that is at the core of the paper—and his own sense of self.

I remember with painful vividness a time when I was in Jon's shoes. Fall of 1966, Oberlin College, Freshman English. For our first graded paper we had to define an abstract concept with specific examples (we had read Aaron Copeland's essay, "What Is Music" as a model—not much help). My fate was probably sealed when I chose the uplifting topic of "courage." My point was that true courage is private and unseen; and that the models of courage often held up in the media were tainted by praise. My two examples were Walter "the Flea" Roberts—a kick returner for the Cleveland Browns who weighed 150 pounds—and Robert E. Lee. I recognize now that using "the Flea" was probably a mistake because Oberlin College treated football with considerably less reverence than did Ashland, Ohio, where football was the generally accepted analogy for life. I can now imagine the bemused look my instructor must have had when he saw tailback and Civil War general hooked up in this evidentiary chain.

My paper was one of two picked and anonymously distributed for a whole-class critique. The first paper, which seemed to be on a much less serious topic than mine (and which had no references to football) was generally praised. But it quickly became apparent that mine was a disaster. If I rose to defend it my authorship would become apparent, so I watched the class pick at it as "obvious" and "trite" and "inadequately supported." When the class ended mercifully at 3:00, the instructor announced that there were some problems in the paper that hadn't yet been dealt with, and the discussion would carry over to Monday.

I'm sure if I could retrieve the paper I would agree with much of the criticism. Yet to be eighteen—on my own, still in awe of John Kennedy, ready to "pay any price, bear any burden"—courage was on my mind. That interest could have been met with greater sympathy. In time, of course, I outgrew the sincere virtuousness that prompted me to write about courage in the first place.

5

Heroes and Antiheroes

Every man in the chapel hoped that when his hour came he, too, would be eulogized, which is to say forgiven, and that all his lapses, greeds, errors, and strayings from the truth would be invested with coherence and looked upon with charity. This was perhaps the last things human beings could give each other and it was what they demanded, after all, of the Lord.
—James Baldwin, "Notes of a Native Son"

In *The Adventures of Tom Sawyer,* Tom and his gang slip off to an island in the river and, after a severe storm, are believed by the townspeople to be drowned. The boys come back into town for their funeral, hiding in the balcony while their eulogy is delivered:

> As the service proceeded, the clergyman drew such pictures of the graces, the winning ways, and the rare promise of the lost lads that every soul there, thinking he recognized these pictures, felt a pang in remembering that he had persistently blinded himself to them always before and had persistently seen only faults and flaws in the poor boys. The minister related many a touching incident in the lives of the departed, too, which illustrated their sweet generous natures, and people could easily see how noble and beautiful those episodes were, and remembered with grief that at the time they had seemed rank rascalities well deserving of cowhide. (Twain [1876] 1946, 167)

Tom's many larcenies, the horrible things he did to cats, are transformed or forgotten in the ceremonial need to construct a positive picture of him.

The eulogy is one of many forms of sentimental discourse that Twain satirizes in this book (school compositions and chivalric romances are two others). Still the selective and stylized presentation in the eulogy serves a real psychological need. From whatever source—a survivor's guilt, a desire to forgive, a sense of loyalty, a need to see life itself as meaningful—we depend upon these occasions to provide us with a memory that sustains us, one in which the sins, complications, and dividedness of human nature are put aside, at least momentarily.

55

In this chapter I look at two deliberately uncomplicated forms of writing that appear in a beginning writing course. I term these testimonials (for the living) and eulogies (for the dead). Each form serves a psychological and developmental need of the writer: they show loyalty, they draw a lesson from the life of someone else, they affirm traditional values, and they are an act of thanks to those who have taken seriously their generational obligation to teach and serve as a model. Yet the very one-dimensional, sometimes sentimental, quality of these forms may clash with an aesthetic that values irony, complexity, and ambiguity. Where eulogies and testimonials seek to construct a coherent positive "self," this picture may seem maudlin and dishonest to those who endorse an aesthetic that prefers the postmodern image of the divided, fragmented self. The tendency then is to deconstruct, to critique, to look for feet of clay.

Several years ago in a workshop I asked the participants to think of a place that mattered to them, and of the people associated with that place. The piece I wrote, which I reproduce unedited below, began as a description of the farm where my mother grew up, but turned into a tribute to my grandfather:

At the end of each visit to my grandfather's farm in northwestern Ohio, he would secretly call me aside, a tilt of the head. He wanted to talk with just me, secretly, in the pantry. I knew what was coming but always felt like a conspirator—we'd have our secret from my parents.

In the pantry, Grampa Schlatter would press a new half-dollar into my palm, "Here's a little something for you." I'd pretend to refuse, the way my mother had taught me to, "Grandpa you don't have to. . . ." But I always said it knowing he would insist, knowing that the half-dollar was mine. Then he would give me a pack of Juicy Fruit gum for the trip home. When I smell that gum today I instantly recall Grandpa, by the pantry, our secret—which of course was no secret at all.

He was a short man, about 5 feet two inches, the shortest adult I knew, stocky and strong; he had an overwhelming handshake that made you flex your fingers afterward. But he was the gentlest man I had ever met. My father could go off on rages (as I now can), but my mother remembers him really angry only once—when she tried to pull one of her teeth with a dirty pair of plyers.

He planted his garden well into his 80s. And what a garden! Once he allowed us to dig up potatoes near the chicken coop. They were huge, the size of softballs. Even when we got a good start on our garden, he was always ahead. "Knee high by the fourth of July." Hardly. His corn stalks were over our heads. The tomatoes were bigger and there were crops we wouldn't try—cantaloupes and radishes. My dad credited the chicken manure, but I wasn't so sure.

These visits were also a holiday for our dog, Hans, a leash dog at home but able to run free on the farm. The second we stopped the car, he was out the door joining Curley, Grampa's burly Spaniel—and later Blackie, my uncle's terrier who ran them both into the ground. Like cousins they'd head off into the woods and come back a couple hours later, tongues hanging, coats full of burrs, and on one occasion smelling of skunk. Sometimes our dog would just bark and bark, disturbing the peace of the farm. "It's OK," Grandpa said, "they have to do it or they'll forget how."

In the house we could feel connections to our ancestors from Switzerland. Under the clock, Grandpa kept old Bibles passed down by the Schlatter family. Each visit my brother and I would look at the ornate penmanship of the signatures. In the upstairs bedroom was a large porcelain pitcher and bowl. My mother said that on severely cold nights the water would freeze in the bowl. The enamel was covered with a lacework of cracks that seemed more beautiful that the original smooth white could ever have been.

Grandpa Schlatter seemed to defeat time for a while. His hair began to turn gray in his 70s, he mowed his lawn with a push mower into his mid eighties, until a slow moving cancer began to take his strength. Near the end his mind became clouded, too. He became obsessed with a bill that he thought he owed a roofer, and would talk about it each time my mom visited him in the nursing home. My Uncle Ed, a plumbing contractor, produced fake bills of sale marked "paid" to ease this worry, but it didn't help.

The year after my grandfather died a tornado set down near the house and moved it off the foundation. (Strange the role of tornadoes in my family—in 1917 a tornado destroyed my father's home, killing his father and sister.) One of my cousins took a picture of the house, sitting awkwardly in the yard. I felt detached as I looked at it; with Grandpa gone it was just another house.

This is hardly a balanced picture of my grandfather. Though he was a great gardener, I'm not sure he was a great farmer. As I think about it, he wasn't a farmer at all when I knew him. Old plows rusted in the sheds around the farm; the chicken coop was unused and unsafe to enter. He'd leased his farmland to one of the local agribusinesses, and he worked in town at a factory that made LaChoy Chinese food. So his story could be a sadder one—of the disappearance of the family farm. Was he a good and loving husband to his invalid wife? I can't say for sure. And, to be honest, I would resist this more complex picture of him.

This is the way I choose to remember him. It is a "sacred" memory. I've chosen to see him as a model of uncomplaining fortitude, of stoicism, that remains for me a standard of behavior. There is also a pastoral dimension to the standard he set, a closeness to the soil and the cycles of growth, that was new and appealing to someone who grew up in a town. In his beautiful poem, "Digging," Seamus Heaney (1980) captures the sense of his own separation from a natural world that both his father and grandfather knew intimately:

> By God, the old man could handle a spade.
> Just like his old man.

His father could handle the potato digging:

> He rooted out the tall tops, buried the bright edge deep
> To scatter the new potatoes that we picked
> Loving the cool hardness in our hands.

His grandfather was an expert turf-cutter who would barely pause for a drink of milk that Heaney, as a young boy, brought him. These memories, like the "living roots" in the bog, come back to him, reminding him that he has "no spade to follow men like them." He will "dig" with his pen. Even this resolution is equivocal, and we are left with the impression that something important is lost when pen substitutes for spade. Yet the standard of work and craft, of digging, "going down and down," was set by those who went before. It is this enabling form of nostalgia that I was trying to convey in my tribute to my grandfather.

For many students, the death of a grandparent is the first intimate look at the last stages of life, and the images are often unforgettable—antiseptic nursing homes, pausing at the threshold of a grandparent's room, the emaciation of cancer, the recognition, as one student put it, that her parents were vulnerable "persons" when she saw their grief. Matthew Brassuer captured these images in a paper he entitled, ironically, "Forgetting." It is a description of his "Memere," who suffered from Alzheimer's disease; it is a memory of someone who could no longer remember. He begins with what is often a set piece in these papers of recollection—entering the hospital (or nursing-home room) and confronting the physical transformation of the grandparent:

> I walked toward the room not knowing what I might find or what might find me. The door was open and I looked in. Nothing was abnormal other than there was only a bed and a few chairs. The bed was on the small side, and there were a great many blankets piled on the bed. That was why I jumped in the air when a voice said, "Come here Bernard." When I looked in the room I had not seen any one there. Now suddenly there was something talking to

me. That something was on, or in, the bed. Possessing an over amount of curiosity like other kids I walked into the room a little farther; even if I was curious I was still nervous about what I might find. I stared at the bed hoping the owner of the voice would make an appearance.

As I got closer it didn't take long for me to notice the small face that was engulfed by the extra fluffy pillows. I looked for confirmation that there was indeed a person there and not just a head. Unfortunately there was no noticeable form in the bed, so thoughts of just a head lying there suddenly began to go through my head. Slowly her face turned to me. She squinted as if she was trying to focus, or maybe she was trying to figure out who I was. "Bernard you have gotten so big," she said in a voice that was muffled by the blankets pulled part way over her face.

"Memere, my name is Matthew," I said this more to myself than to her.

"Matthew, I don't have a grandson named Matthew," she said in a voice that was kind of shaky. At that moment I wanted to be gone. I wanted away from that place. This was not the same lady who one year earlier had almost crushed me to herself in one of the hardest hugs of my life. My father came up behind me and whispered in my ear, "Don't say anything to upset Memere."

Matthew moves on to give some background to the disease and to describe the effect it had upon his father who could only helplessly watch its progression. There was the eventual death, the wake, the funeral, and, according to Brassuer family tradition, the cookout. "The wake and funeral is where we grieve, but the cookout is where we go on with our lives." This cookout provides Matthew with the image of his grandmother that he needs to counterbalance the one with which he began the paper.

Later on in the day during the second helping of dessert we were sitting on the porch of my grandparents' log cabin. It was the men of the family or at least the males of the family that were sitting there. It was about this time that they began to talk about Memere; it was mostly memories and little anecdotes about her. There was one in particular that I remember so well because it shows the contrast in the way she lived and the way she died. . . . It seems that my grandmother was in either Montreal or Quebec, but that is not the point. She is walking down a street and a would-be purse snatcher decided to steal hers. My grandfather said that he picked her because she looked old and in reality she was about 65 but that didn't matter because she worked on the farm and was very strong for her age. Well, the thief came running by her and grabbed her purse, but unlike the usual target she held on and actually pulled the thief off his feet. She then proceeded to give him a beating with the purse that he tried to steal, the whole time she is yelling at him in French, cursing him to no living end. Had the police officer not been close by to pull her off the poor guy she might have seriously hurt him.

After telling this story Matthew comments, "That story was so important because that is how I remember her." With the help of his grandfather he has been able to restore his grandmother not only to the more active women he would like to remember, but to mythic status. He has been given the gift of an emblematic story, dramatic and invariably embellished, which illustrates a trait he chose to remember, one to set beside the horrific image of her—a head without a body—that he used to begin the paper.

Heroes and Mentors

I recently reread *Romeo and Juliet* for an English Methods class I was teaching. I was struck, perhaps because it was for an education class, by the failure of teachers in the play. Both protagonists have a mentor—Juliet her nurse and Romeo Friar Lawrence. But each teacher fails them at a critical moment; Friar Lawrence, too steeped in his own herbal medicine, concocts a scheme that fails because of its complexity. Juliet, working within a much more confined space with far fewer opportunities for advice, must rely on her loving nurse who can't understand why she doesn't marry Paris (such a "man of wax" as she calls him). Their tragedy is rooted in the failure of adults to take seriously the generational responsibilities of mentorship. It is a theme students address as they portray helpful mentors and those who have failed them.

As in the eulogy, one strategy in the testimonial is to find an emblematic story, one which shows in dramatic terms a key moment of instruction. One of my favorite examples was written several years ago by Gina Grassi; in it she describes the bold action of her teacher Mrs. Lawler, which helped shape her own feminism. The incident occurred at a pep rally led by a group of male teachers at her school:

> During one of these infamous pep rallies, some of the men on the teaching staff thought it would be fun, if not inspiring to dress as cheerleaders and cheer for the team. Mrs. Lawler probably could have handled the idea of three grown men parading in front of a mob of screaming kids, wearing mini-skirts and wigs. But when these men blew up balloons and stuck them in their already tight sweaters, Mrs. Lawler was outraged. The straw that broke the camel's back was when one of the teachers, in an attempt to be cute, turned the balloons so that the stems pointed out, achieving the "braless" look.

She flew out of the bleachers and pointed out to the superintendent how immature and disrespectful her male cohorts were being. The superintendent tried to accuse her of taking things too personally and told her she should loosen up a bit. Then she began yelling, "If you think a woman's mammary glands are so funny, would you still be amused if I paraded in front of the student body with a Kielbasa down my pants?"

In her fury, Mrs. Lawler failed to notice that she was still screaming in the direction of the microphone. The entire gym was silent as Mrs. Lawler made her point. The men in the cheerleading outfits were not willing to be humiliated that easily, thus Jill Lawler was dubbed with the nickname, "Jill-basa."

Our English class was happy to hear that story because it took up most of the class time to tell. Mrs. Lawler was justified, however in side tracking this time. I had great admiration for the way she stood up against the whole school. When I heard her being good-naturedly called "Jill-basa" by a fellow staff member, or behind her back by some wise ass student, I have nothing but respect for her.

I believe she actually awakened something inside of me. An inspiration if you will, to believe in myself enough to say what I believe. Out of those hundreds of hours of English classes I have had with Mrs. Lawler, the most valuable lesson I learned was on that day.

Gina's paper deals with the same topic—"life lessons"—that we have seen before (see Jon's paper in the previous chapter), yet she is able to create a narrative structure to this lesson; the scene is set, the conflict occurs, resolves, and causes a change in the writer. There is a before-and-after pattern, hinging on a dramatic moment, in which a new self is defined.

The task may be more difficult for students who cannot mold their experience with a key mentor into this structure, when the key acts of instruction and friendship are habitual and nondramatic. This was the case in the next paper I quote in which a first-semester freshman, a varsity volleyball player, describes Russ, her "boss, advisor, competitor, and friend." It opens with this paragraph:

There are few people that I respect in this world, maybe five, including family. One of these would be my boss, advisor, competitor, and friend. To capture the essence of his character/spirit is a great challenge. But he taught me, "never give up." Maybe he should be writing this, he has such a creative genius of words. He uses his phrase, "something not unlike pleasure in the discomfort of others" to describe the way I speak "tongue in cheek," which is his term for my sarcastic remarks. He uses alliteration often. Despite his profound way with words, he is still looking for one to describe me, although "flibbertigibbet" and "incorrigible" have come up once or twice.

I remember thinking this a promising opening, but I was concerned that it would become a sentimental piece of devotion. And indeed, the ending was a wholehearted, unambiguous recognition of what his friendship had meant:

> Despite all this [their various competitions] we never lose sight of the fact that the only thing that really matters is our friendship. No matter what happens he always takes the time to care. He's always concerned about me and always asking if he can do anything for me or if everything's OK. He's not perfect, obviously because he's a male, but he's as close as any male can get. I've never told him how special he is to me but we've developed an understanding between us. He's come to know me so I don't need to tell him. That's what completes him because understanding is what most people lack in the world.

In the suggestions for revisions I did not tamper with this final paragraph; instead I worked to add incidents or dialogue to help us see Russ, and she later admitted that some of the additions helped:

> Another thing that drives him nuts is this deal we have. When I started working for him he had this annoying habit of repeating the last sentence of everything any one said. It irritated me so I brought it to his attention. Actually I continuously ragged him about it. So, he told me he wanted my help in reforming his verbal habits; every time I caught him repeating someone, he would give me a dime. . . . He gets so defensive now every time I talk to him or make a comment about anything.
> "So, what did you do this weekend?"
> "Jason took me out to dinner."
> "Jason took you out to dinner?"
> "Yes! Jason took me out to dinner. I do believe you owe me a dime."
> "Ahhh! No, I was just confirming what you said. I wasn't sure I heard you correctly."
> "You owe me a dime."

Still Donna wrote in her self-evaluation that Russ is best revealed in a letter he wrote her when she decided to participate in varsity volleyball and consequently had to quit working for Russ on weekends. I remember not being as impressed with this letter as Donna was, but on rereading it I think she's right. In the opening paragraph there is the wordplay we would expect: "Sorry, mustn't pout, for without a doubt, you'll think me a lout and so my character you'll never tout." But he moves into a less playful style as the letter progresses:

I was really glad you called yesterday. I guess we all are somewhat insecure. I cherish our friendship as very unique and special. When your Mom told me your schedule, I began to think (I know, bad idea, being a male) well, if you can't work with me anymore will the friendship fade. I couldn't bear that. Having said that, If you are going to play volleyball, I'll support you totally. I only ask that you keep in touch or I will Pout! Big Time!

You make me laugh and bring a little fun into my long work week. For that, I can't thank you enough. My hope is that you feel comfortable enough to talk to me anytime. I would feel I'd let you down otherwise. . . .

Be Careful and Take Care of Yourself

Russ

As I retype this letter I now find it surprisingly moving and gracious. I think what bothered me at the first reading was the emotional intensity of it, the *unconditional* act of friendship and support. It was like I wanted to back away from the letter, preferring the more displaced way they showed affection through teasing.

Part of the difficulty I had with the essay was its theme of affiliation, the way it endorses the value of friendship—no "news value" there. Rather than presenting herself as an individuated consciousness, Donna celebrates the bond that connects her to her friend. While I am no psychologist, I suspect that affiliation and individuation are complementary needs, the systole and diastole of human development. I don't believe we grow from one to the other; there seems more an alteration. There is also surely a gender difference, in that individuation may be more the path set out for males and affiliation for females—recall that the great male literary hero often confronts his fate alone, in Joyce's words "unheeded, happy, and near the wild heart of nature" ([1916] 1964, 171).

Transgressive Narratives

I'm suggesting (once again) that the aesthetic that guides the reading of papers like Donna's may favor the individuated perspective, the individual set *against* conventional responses and forms of representation. The student who has "voice" or "originality" is often one who can locate the conventional and transgress it through satire or criticism. For the reader, these transgressions provide an illicit pleasure; we enjoy the calculated disrespect. If the testimonial invokes nostalgia, these transgressive narratives free us (writer and reader) from the weight of nostalgia. They liberate us from conventional expectations that age brings a form of wisdom, that nature provides solace, that motherhood is holy. To take an example from fiction, Jane Smiley's

(1991) *A Thousand Acres* seems to evoke, in the opening, a deep-seated belief that farming, particularly family farming, is a wholesome activity (I read my uncles and, of course, my grandfather into the book). Slowly Smiley transgresses this cultural myth; these thousand acres are poisonous, figuratively and literally.

In the papers cited in this section, authors (I believe self-consciously) transgress the conventional ways we are invited to look at patriarchs and matriarchs. According to Erik Erikson (1968), in this late stage in life, a key concern is, or should be "generativity," the "concern for establishing and guiding the next generation" (138). It is the mature sense, as the end of life approaches, that "I am what survives me." It is this quality of generativity that Donna celebrates in the description of Russ. The failure to take on this generational responsibility is the subject of the following transgressive narratives.

Like the family farm, family businesses are part of our cultural mythology, particularly as they become endangered by the generic chain stores. They are visible proof that self-sacrifice and the work ethic pay off, and that the legacy of hard work can be passed on to children. In the opening paragraph of his profile, "Frankie's Drive-In," Matthew DiPentima (1994) begins to distance us from that mythology:

> It is his face, his shirt, his details that still make me mad. They ignite the fire that I quickly douse with a laugh, a laugh tainted with wonderment. The steely hair, forced to its usual place above the protruding eyeballs, cast in shadow by the constantly knit brow. The vertical folds of faintly olive skin around his mouth that came to rest on his cleft chin, like a soft comforter on an unmade bed. This chin became the neck that was finally obscured by a bright crisp collar; below that were two gold Cross pens in their place and ready for the use that seldom came. Mary, Frankie's wife, was the one who pressed this shirt so meticulously. She was short, prim and purposeful, with the same hair, only permed. Her eyes had the added glimmer of compassion, apparently permissible for a grandmother. She had a resigned determination, for she had followed those shiny size eleven wingtips for so long.

What bothered ("ignited") the writer were Frankie's limits—the way he would discriminate against his son's non-Italian girlfriend, the way his children failed to challenge his abuse of authority, and the way his prickliness led to avoidable blowups. In one case, a customer's complaint over a soggy sandwich erupted into profanity and an open fight. The author fought back in the way Frankie's children could not, with the inappropriate smile and smirk, which caused Frankie to create make-work for Matthew that he excused his sons from doing.

As I read this paper, my sympathies, though, are not wholly with Matthew and his quiet way of subversion. And, as it turns out, even he is not fully in sympathy with himself, for he makes a crucial turn in the last paragraph. The summer is over, he has given notice, and returns to claim his check:

> I said my final goodbyes to everybody, and as I passed the office I saw Frankie staring dully from behind the vinyl card table that was his desk. I smiled for the last time. I had won because I had stayed the summer and had not given in. However, I had lost as well. Frankie had made the job very hard and unpleasant, and I was never able to get his family to defend me. I'm glad of that now though. Even though Frankie was a bitter man, I would not want to take his family from him. That is what he had lived for and worked for, and in the end his family understood his faults but remained by him anyway. That to me is comforting because I will not be the smiling kid forever, and I know I will never be perfect.

This last sentence is extraordinary. Up until that point the author had set himself against the small petty world that Frankie had created. And against the reflexive loyalty of wife and children, all of whom seemed to be following those wingtips. Then, in this final sentence, he raises the possibility that he may someday be like Frankie and have to rely on the same kind of forgiving loyalty. It is as if he transgresses the line of respect, then trangresses his transgression by showing some appreciation for the loyalty of the family.

Like Matthew, Meghan Camirand (1995) establishes her intent to transgress in the title of her profile, "My Dad's Mother." She avoids the designation "grandmother" in the title because she wants to announce the antinostalgic tone of her paper. Her father's mother, Doris, was a former mill worker who, in Meghan's eyes, had simply failed as a mother—to the point of placing her father in an orphanage for a year. She neglected his outstanding athletic career, preferring to drink with her "boyfriend" Frank. While her father retains some nostalgic memories of growing up, Meghan works to show the unsubstantial basis for this nostalgia:

> I have pieced together the story of my father's childhood through talks with my dad. Mostly around Christmas he would tell me about one Christmas present, a sled. Yet there was no one there to see him open it; Doris was at Frank's, so the sled stood propped in the doorway, mocking him as he opened up a can of chunky soup for Christmas dinner. I have never forgiven my grandmother for this; my father has.

Meghan undermines the nostalgic intent (Christmas, the gift of a sled) of her father's story, reconstructing the circumstances of the giving.

She is unsparing in her portrait of Doris and Frank. She describes her forced visits to Frank's apartment:

> I hated going there; it smelled of mothballs, cigarettes, and laziness. Her fake leather Barco-lounge chair, rested kitty corner to the front door along with her table and her pack of Marlboros. She wore housecoats and terry-cloth slippers that covered the tops of her pruny feet. She was short. I surpassed her height in sixth grade, and she looked like a big bean bag when she leaned back into the plastic leather. She drank Fresca and said words like "ain't" and "badadoes." Frank's recliner was in the other corner. He would sit there in his skinny, white Hanes tank-top, drinking Cutty Sark, laughing at stupid re-runs of *The Odd Couple*.

Meghan inverts our traditional expectation for a paper about a grandmother, pushing the limits of (justified) disrespect—the human "bean bag" in the matching recliner.

The essay moves on to describe the way Doris is now dependent on her father, who loyally cares for her. Meghan is torn between her own impression of Doris and the way her father, by romanticizing his own past, can maintain a more positive image. In effect, she inverts the developmental progression I've laid out in this chapter: it is the *father* who unconditionally accepts Doris, while the daughter seems to recognize all that the father has to leave out of the picture to do this. Near the end of the paper, in one heartbreaking paragraph, Meghan locates the difference in her father's need to maintain a particular kind of memory, a sacred memory:

> My father claimed that she did the best she could, with what she could. He would then retell the story he always told in my grandmother's defense. During his junior year in high school, she gave him a week's pay to buy the same basketball sneakers as everyone else.
>
> On the third stair of our cellar, next to the Whisk and the mop, are a pair of Chuck Taylor All-Star Converse high tops. They are tattered around the ankles and worn through the toes. They used to be Bozo red but are now the color of fading burn. They aren't the same sneakers my dad had in high school, but they are exact replicas. He says they are the best sneakers he has ever owned. Maybe they represent one of the only memories she gave him. He has for her the unconditional love a child has for his mother, a love so strong that it clouds reality and clings to sentiment associated with chocolate chip cookies and TV families.

Meghan's father retains this one mythic memory, one whole week's wages to buy a pair of Converse high tops. Yet even this recollection seems embroidered —I remember those high tops and they didn't cost that much. Factuality isn't the point though. It fits the master narrative her father constructed—"she did the best she could, with what she could."

Meghan concludes that "time, age, and my father have made me accept my grandmother." But this acceptance does not reach to understanding. She ends with the hope that "Someday, maybe I will see her through his eyes." But this ending seems almost too modest; she has, by looking at the relationship of memory and affection, come a long way toward understanding.

My own "father's mother" led a life that parallels, in some key ways, Meghan's story. Until reading her essay, I had never thought of interrogating it as she does. My grandfather died when a tornado hit New Albany, Indiana, in 1917, and because he had been a paid-up member of the Junior Order of American Mechanics, my grandmother could place her two sons (her daughter also died in the tornado) in an orphanage in Tiffin, Ohio, where she went to work as a laundress. My dad has only fond memories of the orphanage—of the kind patriarch, Dad Kiernan, who ran it, and of his five hundred brothers and sisters. He still goes to the reunions, along with my mother, who taught there. Yet his mother is virtually absent from these stories. Was the orphanage the best choice, the only choice? What was it like to grow up with a mother so present, yet absent? Did this absence of parents have anything to do with the mess my uncle made with his life? Was it the idyllic place my dad describes?

Meghan's father is heroic in her eyes, because he has reversed the generational pattern:

> He has coached softball teams, filmed four-hour cheerleading competitions, presided over PTA meetings. Every Saturday morning, he wakes up to cook a full breakfast: pancakes, French toast, coffee, bagels, and Janet's donuts from Robie's Country Store. I love my father.

I cannot determine the effect my father's lack of parents had on him; I cannot imagine it is as benign as his own story makes it out to be. Yet, he too has reversed the pattern.

There's a picture taken of him at one of my brother's baseball games on a cold evening early in the season. He is sitting on a spectators bench, alone, with a blanket wrapped around him. I picture it as a desultory, walk-filled game, too early in the season and too cold for the pitchers to have much control. Even the hits are painful to the batters. My father looks on, his shoulders hunched in the cold, without much expression. The message of the picture is that he was *there*. He is giving the gift of attendance that had never really been given to him.

Near the end of his brilliant career, the physicist Richard Feynman began to turn his attention toward gravitation; the only problem was that gravity, compared to the forces within the atom, is incredibly weak—the difference an almost inconceivable 10 to the 42d power. In fact, he said during a lecture, "it's *damn* weak." At that moment a loudspeaker broke loose from the ceiling and crashed to the floor. Without missing a beat, Feynman added, "Weak, but not negligible."

To attempt an analogy, it is almost a commonplace among some of the more politically oriented composition theorists to consider personal writing as solipsistic and disempowering when compared to writing that engages issues of race, class, and power. Yet, the writing students do about heroes, mentors, and what Erikson calls generativity, confronts issues of profound significance, of nuclear as opposed to gravitational force. How does a generation prepare the way? And how do we choose to remember that older generation? How do we construct our own narrative in a way that empowers, inspires, and sustains us? What images (Meghan's father making breakfast; mine at the baseball game) do we hold on to? What mythic or emblematic stories do we return to again and again?

Maybe the most eloquent testimony to the power of this type of memory comes in Alyosha's children's sermon at the end of *The Brothers Karamazov*:

> You must know that there is nothing higher and stronger and more whole wholesome and good for life in the future than some good memory, especially a memory of childhood, of home. People talk to you a great deal about your education, but some good sacred memory, preserved from childhood, is perhaps the best education. If a man carries many such memories with him into life, he is safe to the end of his days, and if one has one good memory left in one's heart, even that may be the means of saving us. (Dostoievsky [1865] 1944, 875)

6

In Defense of Pleasure

Speculation: the faculty or power of seeing; sight, vision, esp. intelligent or comprehending vision.

—*Oxford English Dictionary*

On May 18, 1868, William James wrote his friend Oliver Wendell Holmes Jr. from his hotel in Dresden. His letter begins with the typical Jamesian exuberance: "Your unexpected letter has just burst into my existence like a meteor into the sphere of a planet, and here I go to answer while the heat developed by the impact is at its highest" (James 1960). In the middle of the long letter, James provides a vivid sketch of the scene outside the hotel restaurant:

> As I sit by the open window waiting for my breakfast and look out on a line of *Droschkes* drawn up on the side of the Dohna Platz, and see the coachmen, red-faced, red-collared, and blue-coated, with varnished hats, sitting in a variety of indolent attitudes upon their boxes, one of them looking in upon me and probably wondering what the devil I am,—when I see the big sky with a monstrous white cloud battening and bulging up behind the houses into the blue. . . . when I see the houses opposite with their balconies and windows filled with flowers and greenery—Ha! on the topmost balcony of one stands a maiden, black-jacketed, red-petticoated, fair and slim under the striped awning, leaning her elbow on the rail and her peach-like chin upon her rosy fingertips! Of whom thinkest thou, maiden, up there aloft? Here, *here!* beats the human heart for which in the drunkenness of the morning hour thy being vaguely longs, tremulously, but recklessly and wickedly, posits elsewhere, over those distant treetops which thou regardest. (James 1960, 62–63)

This chapter deals with pleasure, more specifically with the relationship of description, that lowliest of modes, to hedonism. In this passage, the reader experiences the perceptual pleasure of a moment. In this correspondence between two young men, on the brink of careers that would transform American intellectual life, it is a romantic still frame, freed of any moralistic intent, free of any serious commentary.

69

The day has in fact begun, and when I see all this and think that at the same moment thou art probably in a dead sleep whirled around through the black night with rocks and trees and monuments like an inanimate thing, when I think all this I feel—*how?*—I give it up myself. (63)

Description of this kind might be viewed as a discourse that resists the generalizing "meaning-making" bias of academic life—and the often-oppressive moralizing discourse that students encounter at about every turn.

Even the rationales for engaging in English Studies have a strongly moralistic flavor, perhaps for good strategic reasons. It would certainly not be in our professional interests to admit that reading a novel might be closer to eating a good meal than to achieving a higher level of moral sensitivity. Rationales for literature and composition typically lay out bold moral and civic claims. The McGuffey readers were unabashedly concerned with moral behavior and citizenship. And this emphasis carries over in more recent rationales for the study of literature and composition. Here, for example, is a statement from Judith Langer's (1995) *Envisioning Literature:*

[The literary imagination] permits us to create new combinations, alternatives and possibilities, to understand characters and situations in ways not necessarily suggested when we take things as they are. It permits us to become fuller, more thoughtful, and more informed members of the world—*in both literature and life.* (8) (emphasis added)

This claim seems modest when compared with some made for socially engaged composition pedagogies. To pick from the most recent copy of *College Composition and Communication,* I quote the conclusion of Richard Marback's (1996) essay, "Corbett's Hand":

By debating the values of an open-handed rhetoric, by contending with terms and conditions of a pedagogy of democratic citizenship, composition studies reproduces and reiterates, at the same time it transforms and critiques, the larger struggles of contemporary American life as they are fought out through social organizations that distribute power and authority according to race, class, and power. (197)

These assertions of moral and civic value claim a utility for our work that no appeal to pleasure could possibly achieve. Such a rationale would surely be perceived as complicit with a consumer culture saturated with the ethic of self-gratification.

In this climate of moral protectiveness, hedonism is perceived as the problem, not as a worthy subject of composition. I suspect that students read this situation and learn to represent their experiences in a morally acceptable way, as progressive narratives of self-actualization. They learn to stress the heightened self-awareness, the extension of sympathy, that literate work engenders. And, not to be cynical, this construction of self has real value for them, as I argued earlier. It can fit an appealing master narrative of self-development.

Yet it leaves out a lot—those nonimproving experiences, the young woman on the balcony ("Here, *here* beats the heart. . . .") In order to make a place for a nonmoralizing celebratory discourse, I want to explore the "spectator" role as developed by essayists like Addison and Steele. I then will show how one of William James' colleagues, Barrett Wendell (who actually taught James' sons), created a place for this role in his composition courses.

The Spectator

The stance of spectator was popularized by Joseph Addison and Richard Steele who wrote and published a periodical with that name in the early eighteenth century. To begin to define the self-presentation of the spectator, it might be useful to contrast it with the way a writer like George Orwell locates himself in "Shooting an Elephant":

> In Moulmein, in Lower Burma, I was hated by large numbers of people—the only time in my life that I have been important enough for this to happen to me. ([1936] 1988, 768)

Within the one sentence Orwell condenses the theme of the essay, the paradox of "importance." From the first sentence, there is the insistence not only that there is a moral significance to his essay, but that he will be at the center of this significance. He pictures himself as engaged, fully employed in the dirty work of empire-maintenance. His approach is self-dramatizing, as if *his own* self-development, his resolution of the paradox of the opening sentence, is centrally important for the reader.

The spectator makes no such claim. Rather than calling attention to the significance of the writing subject, there is an attempt to minimize, even mock, the writer's importance. The writer is an "idler," a "tattler," a "rambler" seemingly without any permanent or significant form of employment. Someone with time to fill. As Richard Steele ([1710] 1994) writes in the opening to "Twenty-four Hours in London":

> It is an inexpressible Pleasure to know little of the World, and be of no Character of Significancy in it.

This, to be sure, is something of a pose—Steele, by virtue of his writing, *was* a figure of some "significancy." And there is no question that he knew London.

According to Steele, the motive for this form of writing is perceptual pleasure:

> To be ever unconcerned, and ever looking on new Objects with an endless Curiosity is a Delight known only to those who are turned to Speculation: Nay, they who enjoy it, must value things only as they are Objects of Speculation, without drawing any worldly Advantage to themselves from them, but just as they contribute to their Amusement, or the Improvement of Mind. (129)

This being the case, Steele explains why he should be excused for greeting complete strangers on the street:

> This is a Particularity would be tolerated in me, if they considered that the greatest Pleasure I know I receive at my Eyes, and that I am obliged to an agreeable Person for coming abroad into my View, as another is for a Visit of Conversation at their own Houses. (129)

Speculation, as Steele uses the term, is primarily a visual capacity, an alertness to what Ken Macrorie (1970) would call, 250 years later, "fabulous realities." The key unit in the spectator piece is often a short vignette, sometimes less than a paragraph.

Virginia Woolf's "Street Hauntings" is an example of the genre. The piece begins ostensibly with Woolf needing to go to the store for a pencil, and it becomes a series of sharp, brief pictures of the "maimed company" that wander London streets. In just a few sentences she catches the march of two blind brothers:

> Two bearded men, brothers, apparently, stone-blind, supporting themselves by resting their hand on the head of a small boy between them, marched down the street. On they came with the unyielding yet tremulous tread of the blind, which seems to lend to their approach something of the terror and inevitability of the fate that had overtaken them. As they passed, holding straight on, the little convoy seemed to cleave asunder the passersby with the momentum of its silence, its directness, its disaster. ([1942] 1994, 259)

Though Woolf poignantly describes what she sees, wondering where these derelicts sleep, there is no social commentary, certainly no consideration of ethics or social policy. The purpose of her observation is "delight and wonder"—"to escape is the greatest of pleasures" (265).

At the end of Steele's twenty-four hours in London he returns to his room to review his notes:

When I came to my Chamber I writ down these Minutes; but was at a Loss what Instruction I should propose to my Reader from the Enumeration of so many insignificant Matters and Occurrences; and I thought it of great Use, if they could learn with me to keep their Minds open to Gratification, and ready to receive it from any thing it meets with. This one Circumstance will make every Face you see give you the Satisfaction you now take in beholding that of a Friend; will make every Object a pleasing one; will make all the Good which arrives to any Man, an Increase of Happiness to yourself. (Steele [1710] 1994, 132–33)

In a sense nothing happens to Steele that changes him in the way Orwell was changed; there is no insight, no increased self-awareness. The "self" here is a fairly stable (if "insignificant") point of observation. He doesn't become a "better" person—to begin to make that claim would be to take himself much too seriously. The only change that does occur is "an Increase of Happiness," the gratification of observing a world so varied and particularized that it is irreducible into any lesson of instruction.

The spectator stance, as defined by Steele and others, lifts the burden of "significance" and replaces it with the hedonistic goal of pleasure or happiness. In doing so it dramatically opens the field of topics for writing. If our minds are "open to Gratification" we will "make every Object a pleasing one." This pleasure is rooted in perception more than conception, in the visual more than the intellectual, in looking outward more than inward, in amusement and delight more than in self-improvement. The two great advocates on this spectator stance in the history of composition instruction were Barrett Wendell and Ken Macrorie.

"To Feel What Life Is"

In many ways Barrett Wendell is a curious model for contemporary composition teachers: an Anglophile, a manic-depressive, a dandy, an elitist with class prejudices that made even Harvard President Eliot cringe. In the classroom he could be caustic and intimidating. Yet the English 12 course he designed for Harvard juniors in the mid 1880s was wildly popular, a virtual rite of passage, taken by approximately 80 percent of a typical class of 250. Wendell also left a remarkably complete record of his teaching—class notes, grade books, and over six thousand student themes.

On the posthumous publication of Wendell's letters, H. L. Mencken wrote:

Wendell got rid of the narrow bookishness, still lingering in Lowell. He was primarily a critic, not of literary manners and postures, but of human existence under the Republic. . . . He did not bury his nose in books; he went out and looked at the world, and what he saw there amused him immensely and filled him with ideas. ([1926] 1977, 248)

One of Wendell's goals as a writing teacher was that his students go out and look at the world. He began his 1888–89 class with this exhortation:

So far as I can stimulate you and you one another to feel what life is; to feel the inevitable inadequacy of all expression thereof; to feel, more and more, the beauty for all its inadequacy, of the great expressions that have been made for us—the ugliness and vileness of the mean one;—we shall do well. We shall help one another to gain from this work training that will make us if not better writers at least better men. (Notes on Lectures, October 3, 1888)

Like the rationales quoted earlier, Wendell asserts that writing can lead to human improvement. But this improvement comes from a heightened capacity "to feel what life is," a capacity that mere bookishness, what students then called "grinding," could not nurture. As Mencken said, it was necessary to go out and look at the world. Indeed any representation of "life" is only an approximation of something that is far greater.

To engage students in this work Wendell needed to stigmatize the sententious style, the chaining of moral commonplaces that had long been the favored writing at Harvard (in the pre-Eliot years many Harvard graduates became ministers), and remained popular in the high schools that fed Harvard during Wendell's time. In his classes "moralizing" became a term of rebuke. Wendell invented the "daily theme" as a method of "cultivating the powers of observation" and developing the habit of forceful writing. Each day (excepting Sunday) students would write about 150 words on something that occurred during that day (they were cautioned to avoid recollections). Simple multiplication testifies to the importance Wendell and his assistants placed on the daily theme; 180 students, each writing 200 daily themes equals 36,000 themes a year. Even students commented on the time-consuming task of this reading; one wrote, "How pitiful it must be for a man to peruse 200 odd sermons [daily themes] every day, week after week, and worst of all, like the Shades in Hades, not be permitted to die" (Wendell 1886, 1887).

At first read, these themes are so simple and direct that they appear slight, and after reading through fifty or sixty (a fraction of a day's work for Wendell) they can feel numbingly repetitive. In fact, "the weather" became such an overused topic that instructors blacklisted it, causing one student to lament that "the weather has always been my short anchor." The challenge for me was to reconstruct Wendell's act of reading—what was he after in these glimpses of student life? What kind of audience was he?

A clue, though a cryptic one, is the single word comment he would make on the back. Terms of criticism focus on vagueness, generality, and an abstractness that lacked "force"—"diffuse," "heavy," "windy," "a little formal," "labored," "moralizing." By contrast his terms of praise focus on an almost casual simplicity and directness: "sensible," "vivid," "simple," "sympathetic," "easy," "colloquial." Despite the intimidating reputation Wendell cultivated, the writer-reader relationship in these accounts is sometimes direct and intimate, close to what James Britton et al. (1975) would call "student-to-trusted-adult." It is as if Wendell restored youthfulness to the students he taught, or at least made a place for youthfulness in the writing. It is difficult, after reading these themes, to realize these students were the same age as those who wrote the more formal essays that had been the norm.

Students would, for example, write about dorm life, a topic that fascinated Wendell since his own college days at Harvard:

> Systematic grinding is the rule. At any rate it is at 21 H'ke [Holyoke], and my chum and myself have settled right down to a thorough review of the term's work. There he sits in his corner hard at work under his student's lamp, and I am in the adjoining room doing the same. We have our gas turned down in order to give a scholarly air to our occupation, as well as to let our friends know they have broken in on a grinding party. At first we found it rather hard to study together, as we always had a great deal to say to each other. My chum would suddenly break out after a long silence with: "What bully eyes Marse *has* got, hasn't she?" or I would exclaim suddenly after we had been quietly studying for half an hour, "Well, by gosh, I got nine goals out of eleven tries today!" This sort of thing we have now entirely overcome, and get on without interruption for hours together. (Wendell 1886, 1887)

The same writer strikes the "observer" pose in this description of a practical joke:

> One evening last June, as I was returning from dinner, I noticed in the distance a lot of students. As I was much engaged in reading a letter I quite passed over the event until I was almost upon them. Then the loud laughing and general look on every body's face attracted me. The college men, who had gathered to the number of twenty or more, called me to come where they were. I did so. Upon looking upwards towards the top of Hilton Block my eyes fell upon a huge card which hung out of a friend's window. On the cards were these words: "Girls Wanted." It was, of course, a joke played by those below, and created much fun in the square. As the owner of

the room in question was one of unusually immaculate character, and a candidate for the freshmen crew, I thought it a good joke.

Students soon discovered that in order to come up with 200 topics for themes, it was necessary to look beyond the dormitory, as in this description of an amputation at the medical school:

This morning I saw evidence of what science will do. It was an almost blood-less amputation. It was the first time I had even seen one, and I was much moved by the skill displayed. The man's foot was so effected that it had begun to mortify, and amputation of this part was found necessary. The foot was first tightly bandaged with rubber which caused the blood to flow into the legs and body, then an arrangement was placed around the leg at the knee which stopped the flow lower than the knee. The result was that doctors could operate without being impeded by the flowing blood, and the opera-tion was really not at all unpleasant. After the amputation the veins were carefully tied, the skin replaced, and the ugly wound entirely covered over.

At times these themes could be surprisingly gentle, even sentimental. During the 1886–87 term, electric lights were installed in Harvard Yard, re-placing the much dimmer gas lights. One student complained of the change:

Last night I noticed perhaps for the first time the effect in the yard of the new electric lights, and I must acknowledge that I am not pleased. I am very conservative in my feeling, and where a change is not necessary as of decided advantage, I had much rather it should not be made. It has always seemed to me that there was an addition of interest in the picturesque gloom (if I may use an adjective to describe the sentimental feelings awak-ened) which settled over Harvard's halls at night. Something as though Alma Mater was personified, and as though the student in entering the yard from the lighted thoroughfare, came within the mouth of her protection, into which the busy public could not even see. In other words as if the yard were the home of Alma Mater, which was more clearly defined by the dark-ness in contrast to the lights of the street.

But this is changed. The beams of the electric lights penetrate way across the yard, light up her semi-private retreats and in this additional way cause her to approach the link of the public.

Pieces like this suggest that students felt a measure of safety in Wendell's often confrontational class. Though he does seem to apologize for his use of the sentimental adjective "picturesque"—in response, no doubt, to some Wen-dell stricture on the direct representation of experience.

The most controversial daily theme written during the 1886–87 term used as a "point of departure" DeQuincey's *Confessions of an Opium Eater,* a required text for the class. The theme was a careful description of smoking a joint of opium, and was read aloud by Wendell as an example of forceful writing. The theme, unfortunately, was not saved, but student reactions appeared in subsequent daily themes. One student wrote appreciatively that he could now see the difference between two of Wendell's key terms, "force" and "elegance":

> The theme we read today on opium smoking showed very clearly the difference. The theme had, to me at least, more force than any that has been read. I could see the opium joint plainly as the writer described the minute details. (Wendell 1886, 1887)

Clearly, opium use was not uncommon in the 1880s for even relatively minor pain. And Wendell's friend, William James, was publicly experimenting with the role of "nitrous oxide" in producing altered states of consciousness. Still, it must have been a shock for the young congregationalists in Wendell's class to read a student account of opium smoking—without *any* accompanying moral warning. Wendell seemed to allow this topic as a legitimate one, which provoked this protest:

> It is surprising that anyone should write a theme like the one read in class this morning giving an account of his first experience and unpleasant sensations he had when he first tried that pernicious practice, opium smoking. I had supposed before that no matter how low-minded or low-lifed any man was that he would hardly have the courage to force such a theme, as that I heard this morning, on the public. Even if it had been beautifully written, it would not be acceptable to the majority of its readers. If a man has an idea that he can write as well or even better than DeQuincey the sooner he gets that out of his head the better.

This response exemplifies the sanctimoniousness, the church-bred orthodoxy, that Wendell tried to undermine and provoke. This ready-made morality presented a barrier to the open experience of the world, a "loss of the creature." In this context, to become a nonmoralizing spectator, alert to visual possibilities, could be seen as a form of liberation.

Fabulous Realities

Early in *Telling Writing,* Ken Macrorie (1970) reproduces a student paper that represents for him "honest" writing. Included in his section on "Telling Truths," it begins:

Thundering down a Northern Michigan highway at night I am separated from the rest of the world. The windows of the car are all rolled down and the wind makes a deep rumbling as the car rises and falls with the dips in the pavement. The white center lines come out of the darkness ahead into the beams of the headlights only to disappear again under the front edge of the hood. . . . I put more pressure on the pedal under my foot; the bar moves up to 100 . . . 110. The lines flash faster and the roar of the wind drowns the noise of the crickets and the night. (7)

Macrorie's short commentary at the end of the paper suggests the stance he is asking us to take as readers and teachers:

This boy may have been driving at an immorally high speed—even for a relatively uninhabited region—but he was writing morally, because he was staying true to the feel of his experience. (8)

Conceivably Macrorie could have picked a different example to place in this important spot in his book, one which does not raise the issue of the moral behavior of the writer. Yet, like Wendell with the smoking of the opium joint, he tries to be provocative, to mock the moral conventionality that would meet this vivid writing with a lecture on car safety.

Like Wendell, Macrorie takes one additional outrageous step by hijacking the language of morality for his cause. Students are to strive not for "accuracy" or "exactness" but "truth." Wasting words is a "form of dishonesty." A style that conveys "the feel of experience" is not merely effective but "moral." To write immorally, then, is to adopt a generalized, conventionalized style— "Engfish" in a memorable coinage he borrowed from a student—that stood as a barrier between the writer and the experiential world. It creates a perceptual fog.

Though Macrorie does not go so far as to acknowledge that language inevitably fails to capture "what life is," he does, like a true romantic, see this capacity as undermined by the desire to use impressive adult language—"As a child [the writer] spoke and wrote honestly most of the time, but as he reaches fifteen honesty and truth come harder" (6). Rather than the casual, underemployed spectator, the writer Macrorie describes is a *witness* with the moral responsibility of accurate description.

Macrorie begins his section on "fabulous realities" with an exhortation that seems lifted from Wendell's opening speech to his students:

Most of us go through each day looking for what we saw yesterday and we find it, to our half-realized disappointment. But the man who daily expects to encounter fabulous realities runs smack into them again and again. He keeps his mind open for his eyes. (37)

The mind is a servant for the eyes, for *speculation* in that original sense of the term. And even though he has made the standard rhetorical move of connecting literacy with morality, it is clear from his examples that perceptual pleasure is at the heart of his method. His examples, and the ones I include, raise interesting questions about self-presentation. To what extent are his students "juvenilized" by this approach? By praising "honest" descriptions of what might seem immature behavior, are we, as readers, complicit in it? How much like adults should student writers appear?

I want to examine these questions by looking at several papers written to an assignment I drew from Macrorie's "People Talking" section. As a model for the assignment we read excerpts from a master of the spectator role, Joseph Mitchell, who had a lifelong affection for gypsies, street corner preachers, saloons, and eating establishments of New York City. Here he shows the surliness of clammers:

> "Hello Pop," a young clammer said to the man in an adjoining boat, a sullen old man in wet overalls, "how's your hammer hanging?" "Shut up," said the old man. "Didn't get your fair share of clams today, did you, Pop?" "Shut up!" said the old man. "Why, hell, I was just passing the time of day." "Shut up!" said the old man. (1993, 311)

We read several examples from Mitchell, and I asked students to be alert to conversations in their dorms, with friends, particularly those that showed, like Mitchell does here, the eccentricity or weirdness of those talking. These could be extended conversations or brief snatches—they did not need to be full narratives. Some, like this phone conversation, resembled the short "fabulous realities" in Macrorie's text:

> "Hello."
> "Hi, is John there?"
> "No, sorry you have the wrong number."
> "A John doesn't live there?"
> "No, John doesn't live here! You have the wrong number!"
> "What number have I reached?"
> "Why does it matter, you have the wrong number!"
> "Is this 595-0729?"
> "Yes, but no John lives here. You have the wrong number!"
> "How can John not live there if I dialed the right number?"
> "I don't know, I don't care, and I don't have time for this! Good-bye!"
> "Gees, I guess I got the wrong number!"

Writing like this has very much the flavor of Wendell's daily themes. But what struck me most about the dialogue assignment was the way it freed many students from writing about serious topics and opened the way to a kind of dailiness, to the pleasure that they took in routine contact with friends, roommates, classmates. They presented a self I had only seen in glimpses before—loud, profane, disrespectful, humorous.

> "Hey Lupa, what kind of music would you do it to?" I asked.
>
> It was Monday night, the kind of night when everyone tried to hold onto the laziness of the weekend by doing anything but homework. My roommates Lupa and Christine had just finished making cupcakes and we were sitting around the kitchen table waiting for them to be done.
>
> She blushed, giggled, and said softly, "Well there's the song by The Who. . . . Do you know The Who?"
>
> "The what?" said my roomate Karen. "Sorry I couldn't resist," and we all laughed. "I wanna do it to show tunes or movie dialogue . . . Hear Dr. Lecter in the background going 'A census taker once tried to test me with these. I ate his liver with some fava beans and fine Chianti . . . fth, fth, fth.' "
>
> "Led Zeppelin holds a special place in my heart 'cause I lost my virginity to it. Pearl Jam's cool, too," I said with a certain air of authority, being the only nonvirgin in a room full of them. . . .
>
> "Have you christened Frank [Frank Sinatra] yet?"
>
> "Not yet," I said as I laughed. "The 'Doobie doobie do' doesn't get me in the mood."

As they eat the half-cooked cupcakes the conversation shifts to fantasies of playing Rizzo in *Grease*, to high school drinking, to playing Pictionary, to squatting and peeing:

> "I can never squat over a toilet bowl. I'm not used to it. I can squat all the way down from being a catcher but I can't do it halfway."
>
> "I bet it's really hard to pee with roller skates on," Christine added.
>
> We laughed, "Yeah, that would be pretty funny," I said imagining it in my head.
>
> "But you know, it's easy when you're skiing 'cause the ski boots hold you up," Lupa said.

The paper ends with them going to sleep, having managed to "hang on to the laziness of the weekend."

Mike DeGrande's paper "Dinner Time" similarly captures the sexualized talk of a group of friends as they prepare to meet Miss New Hampshire in the dining hall. The main character is Geo, who is convinced she will sit with them at dinner. The narrator is not so sure:

"Geo, you know that we're going to rush over there and she ain't going to be there, or we'll see her and she won't be alone. She's tooling with you."

Geo is unconvinced. On the way over Geo decides to check his mailbox:

"For what," I said. "You haven't got mail since you've been at school. Your friends call—remember. They don't know how to write."

In the dinner line Geo is excited about the meal:

"Oh yaaaa. Fuckin' linguine and clam sauce. Oh yaaaa. And meatballs too. They knew I was coming to dinner tonight baby. Can you put a little gravy on that please?"

"I know he's hungry and all but sometimes he's such a creamcake," replied Ross in a deep voice. "I hate when people call sauce 'gravy.' I don't know but it bothers the hell out of me. Like when chicks call underwear 'panties.' I hate the fuckin' word."

They sit down and spot Miss New Hampshire across the dining hall. The narrator bets Geo twenty-five dollars that she walks right by and doesn't say a word.

Miss New Hampshire placed her napkins on her tray and looked around for friends, or possibly for Geo. Her blond hair wavered as she turned her head. She finally smiled and picked up her tray. I couldn't believe she was walking toward us. You have to be kidding me I thought to myself. There is no way in hell she is going to sit with Geo. Oh please keep walking, don't stop. She was walking straight toward our table. Geo corrected his slouching position, and looked at me and smiled. Keep walking, I thought to myself, keep walking.

"Hi, how ya doing?" Geo said, but Miss New Hampshire walked right by. She didn't even pause for a second. As far as she was concerned he wasn't even alive. We all began to laugh.

"Oh shit Geo she fucked your ass. Twenty-five bucks. You're fucked," Ross said as he stopped laughing only to rub it in.

"Geo what did I say to you before? I know you don't remember so I'll tell you. I said that she was tooling you and what did she just do? She gave you the biggest Heisman I have ever seen. She didn't even stop," I said trying to keep laughter in.

"I don't know what I was thinking," Geo said as he shoveled linguine in his mouth. With his head in his plate he smirked and said, "She's really not even that good looking."

At once we all began to laugh. Food flew out of our mouths as we laughed uncontrollably. When I regained my composure I said, "Hey fellas, beers are on Geo tonight." We all began to laugh again. We were all enjoying college, although maybe not Geo.

When the University of New Hampshire instituted a writing requirement, I don't think they had papers like these two in mind. I even expect those who argue for the personal essay would see these as unserious and perhaps immature. But if these papers are ruled inadmissable, why is that? What expectations about self-presentation do they seem to violate?

Writing of this type is removed from any moralizing sphere (though DeGrande seems to be making some judgment about Geo). It is rooted in the pleasure of communal living in a dormitory. This is not grist for self-analysis, or for an exploration of sexual roles—that would be to negate the celebratory mood of the pieces.

Part of this pleasure is sexualized talk, which may appear crude in the increasingly prudish climate of English departments. I remember one instructor lamenting that he was teaching a section on gender, but what his students were *really* interested in was sex. In my experience, they are skeptical of attempts by colleges acting *in loco parentis* to regulate speech. They often enjoy the rawness, the sexual innuendo (a main feature of the wildly popular show *Friends*), and should it get out of hand would prefer to handle the problem themselves. Writing of this kind allows that sexualized underlife into the classroom.

And maybe some of the pleasure students take is in being allowed to "act their age." The great strain of college writing is to appear much older and wiser, to assume a wisdom and judiciousness that seems wildly beyond the reach of an eighteen-year-old. A student who begins a history paper as follows is playing an adult role:

> Slavery did exist in early America. There is no debate about that, but to what extent is the question.

It is October 12 in an introductory course and she speaks as if she is comfortably knowledgeable in the field, already a historian defining what the "question" is. It is a pose—we've all been there. This learning by approximation, what David Bartholomae (1985) calls "inventing the university," is unquestionably a part of how we develop as writers.

Yet there is a danger as well, a developmental insensitivity that seeks to impose a middle-aged "subjectivity" upon relatively young writers. I am frequently stunned by the goals some writing teachers set for their courses—for students to "interrogate their subject position," to understand how discourse "writes" them. I think that it took me most of my undergraduate education to even begin to think in these self-critical terms. By contrast it seems simplistic to claim a place for observation, description, and dialogue. The very fact that "naïve" is often the supreme term of rebuke suggests that acting young can be dangerous.

Sunlight floods the large maple tables in the reading room of the Harvard Archives, hardly the image I had before I went there. I leaf through the indexes and call up the sets of daily themes that Wendell had placed there. I can still see the crease where they were folded a century ago, before being placed in a box at his office. I have come to like these casual communications, and soon the voices of these students merge with voices of my own:

> I always try to write daily themes on something that I have observed during the day. But during the examination period this is hard to do. To-day I hav'nt seen anything but the inside of text books, which would not be very interesting to describe.
>
> The difficulty is increased by the fact that a friend has just come back from a call where he has partly learned a new piece on the banjo. He is trying to pick it out now, but only succeeds in getting a strain here and there. My chum is taking a short rest from grinding, during which he is drumming on the piano. All of these facts, noise from the banjo and piano, and that I haven't observed anything today, make it difficult for me to write. (Wendell 1886, 1887)

I stop occasionally and wander among the class directories, and come across the one for 1889, though compiled much later. I read about the lives of the students whose themes I've just finished. For most, Harvard was the end of formal education. Many returned to the small towns they came from, often to take on the family business. I read about marriages, children, grandchildren, hobbies, their civic and political associations—and their deaths. Because they had, of course, all died.

It was eerie to read the themes, then to walk across the room and read the obituaries. It was as if these students had lived their lives in the time it took me to cross the room, as if the reel of their lives ran forward in those minutes. I suppose a trained archival researcher becomes accustomed to this. But I felt strangely shaken and sentimental when I read these class directories, and grateful to Wendell for preserving something of their life at Harvard, grateful to him for allowing young men to write like young men.

7

Composition Wars and the Place of Personal Writing

Who Publishes doubt and calls it knowledge; Whose Science is Despair...

—William Blake

In his first novel, *Mohawk,* Richard Russo (1986) introduces two sisters, who late in life became intimate friends by strategically creating memories:

> They hadn't been particularly close until the four sisters between them in age died. Since then, the two women began rewriting their pasts until both believed that they had spent every day of their girlhood in each others exclusive company, when in reality the decade and a half that separated their births had made them relative strangers. But they unburdened themselves of this constraining reality for the sake of the vivid, shared recollections that lacked even the slightest basis in fact. (14)

These fabricated memories had the pragmatic value of reconstructing a friendship that "in reality" was never constructed in the first place.

This is pragmatism in its extreme, even caricatured form. The term itself, of course, comes from William James via Charles Peirce, and it might best be viewed not as an "ism," a coherent philosophical system, but as an anatomy of human decision making. In James there was always the predisposition to judge the viability of beliefs by their consequences for human action and human happiness.

Ideas are "true" not because they "mirror" some unchanging external reality; they are true to the extent that they can work as live hypotheses in our lives, to the extent that they have, in James' words, "cash value":

> The truth of an idea is not a stagnant property inherent in it. Truth *happens* to an idea. It *becomes* true, is *made* true by events. Its verity *is,* in fact, an event, a process: the process namely of its verifying itself, its veri-*fication.* Its validity is the process of its valid-*ation.* (1896, 161)

Or to put it in more biblical terms: "By their fruits ye shall know them, not by their roots" (1902, 21).

In James' (1902) most extended pragmatic work, *Varieties of Religious Experience,* he cites testimonies from a range of devout practitioners—mystics, saints, ascetics—to demonstrate the profound and varied "fruits" of religious experience:

> Not God, but life, more life, a larger, richer, more satisfying life, is, in the last analysis, the end of religion. The love of life, at any and every level of development, is the religious impulse. (497)

Using this criteria, religion is vindicated (from attacks by materialistic science) even if "she be without intellectual content, and whether, if she have any, *it be true or false*" (emphasis added). In fact, the "true or false" question, the question of "representation," is irrelevant to human needs. Or as Richard Rorty (1979) would argue eighty years later, "the notion of 'accurate representation' is simply an automatic and empty compliment which we pay to those beliefs which are successful in helping us do what we want to do" (11).

It should be apparent that I have tried to use Jamesian pragmatism in this book to justify forms of personal writing in terms of their consequences for student development. In this chapter I draw again on James to address the challenges of critics of personal writing, particularly those writing as leftist advocates of cultural studies—Alan France, James Berlin, Pat Bizzell, John Trimbur. It is a debate that, in my view, has not been thoughtfully engaged, with exchanges marked by caricature and denigration (see Hairston 1992 and the various responses to her essay). Pragmatism, however, creates a common ground for the exploration of differences. Both pragmatism and the postmodern theories that underlie cultural studies are antifoundationalist; both claim that the question of representation is unanswerable and irrelevant. "Truth" is provisional, culturally bound, in Dewey's words "instrumental."

The Unique Self

Voice. Since I've turned forty, I have begun to call in phone messages to myself. Something occurs to me at home, I call my voice-mail address at school, and leave a message for myself often schizophrenically concluding with a "Thanks" and once a "See you soon." When I listen to this message to myself, I'm often startled. This is not my voice, I think. This sounds like my brother, the same slowness, deliberateness, the hint of fatigue. Or is it my father? For a moment I feel by sense of identity assaulted; *my voice,* this manifestation of self, this aural signature, so very like that of other males in my family.

The critique of personal writing begins with a challenge to this romantic conception of "self"—a coherent, stable, active "essence" that the individual, through an act of sincerity (or "honesty"), can be represented in language. To the extent that a piece of discourse accurately represents this essence it is "authentic." Even the language itself, though obviously shared with others, is sometimes described as "owned" by the writer. I quote from Don Murray's most recent book, *Crafting a Life: In Essay, Story, and Poem,* to suggest the claim now under attack:

> The fear of exposure by writing is a rational fear. But in the act of exposure, writers discover themselves. I meet myself on the page and after decades of writing have come to accept myself—I'd better—and in the process of writing I have learned who I am—and have found a person with whom I can live and work, a person I keep needing to rediscover. (1996, 3)

The root metaphors here—"exposure," "discovery," "found"—suggest a fixed individual essence, a secularized soul, hidden from the individual due to a timidity that prevents the full deployment of language. "Honest" writing allows for the reckoning and healing self-acceptance Murray describes. This "self" is revealed through language but not constituted by language because it exists (hidden) prior to the use of language.

In other words, Murray seems to take a foundational view described by Berlin as follows:

> The existent is located within the individual subject. While the reality of the material, the social, and the linguistic are never denied, they are considered significant only in so far as they serve the needs of the individual. All fulfill their true function only when being exploited in the interests of locating the individual's authentic nature. Writing can be seen as a paradigmatic instance of this activity. It is an art, a creative act in which the process—the discovery of the true self—is as important as the product—the self discovered and expressed. (Berlin 1980, 484)

This is not an unfair representation of what appears to be the epistemological position Murray takes. It also seems a *reductio ad absurdum* that exposes the obvious problems with the position.

- How can this self exist prior to language?
- Isn't the very concept of self a cultural product?
- In what way is this self distinct if our only way of knowing it is through language with conventional meanings?

- As Murray notes elsewhere, doesn't "genre" serve as a lens that limits what we see?
- How can we know that this self is "exposed" honestly, that we're not lying or playing a role? Is honesty anything more than the feeling of being honest?
- If part of this self is the relatively inaccessible "unconscious" how can we claim to fully present ourselves?

According to postmodern critiques, these problems with expressivist epistemological assumptions raise doubts about autobiographical writing. Joe Harris (1987) writes, "It is easy to see, then, why so many students are baffled or intimidated when we ask them to write about what they really know" (161). Faigley (1992) argues that, "To ask students to write authentically about the self assumes that a unified consciousness can be laid out on the page" (127). And, of course, it can't. (One is tempted to ask how a pedagogy, so internally inconsistent, so baffling and intimidating to students, gained the predominance that prompts this critique.)

William James' "fruits not roots" approach shifts the question from epistemology to a pragmatic look at consequences. Suppose, James might argue, that we read Murray and other expressivists as storytellers, creating fictions about the writing process. They are not writing philosophy but a form of exhortation. The test of this method is not in the "truth" of the stories (the roots), but in their capacity to enable students to write with commitment and pleasure, and indirectly to foster values we view as ethical (the fruits). The ease with which critics like Faigley have dismissed terms like "self," "authenticity," and "individual" is startling. Granted that no self can be completely rendered (thus ending the need to keep writing), these concepts—even as fictions—have played such a role in the stories we tell of human development that their utility (and limitations) need a more serious look.

Consequences

The case against expressive pedagogy in many ways resembles Plato's case against the poets in his *Republic*. According to Eric Havelock (1963), Plato was concerned that the epic poets transmitted values in a way that did not make them subject to critical thought. Values were absorbed through the more impulsive process of emulation; the case is similar to the ones made against rock lyrics today. Without some dialectic process focusing on the definition of key terms like "the good," art exerts a covert act of manipulation. Plato's method provided a form of critical protection. This sense of the need for critical protection pervades Plato's dialogues—note how young Phaedrus is "rescued" from the sophist, Lysias.

It is precisely this protective note that is sounded by critics like Alan France (1993). Students, according to France, are "subjects" of a mass youth culture, "in which the self is fashioned out of electronically reproduced images of commodity consumption." The expressive pedagogies are complicit in this inculcation: "the expressivist composing process reinforces the private enjoyment of status and material gratification as the primary values of life" (595).

James Berlin acknowledges that at one level expressivism seems in opposition to institutional discourse and conventions—recall Wendell reading the essay on smoking opium. Yet focus on individualism, on "ownership" of the writing process, and on "free" selection of topics, according to Berlin, allows for this pedagogy to be co-opted by those who promote capitalism. If advertisers can take Janis Joplin's "Lord, Won't You Buy Me a Mercedes Benz?" and turn it into an *advertisement* for Mercedes, what can they do to Donald Murray and Ken Macrorie? Berlin (1988) writes:

> Expressionist rhetoric is easily co-opted by the very capitalist forces it opposes. After all this rhetoric can be used to reinforce the entrepreneurial virtues capitalism most values: individualism, private initiative, the confidence for risk taking, the right to be contentious with authority (especially the state). It is indeed not too much to say that the ruling elites in business, industry, and government are most likely to nod in assent to the ideology inscribed in expressionist rhetoric. (487)

"Individualism" becomes equated with solipsism (Miller 1990, 100), with racism and general intolerance (Bleich 1990, 167), and with isolation (Bauer 1990, 389); it is "debilitating" (Berlin 1988, 491) because it denies communitarian values and resists collective social action. Consequently, as Ronald Strickland (1990) argues, there is a moral responsibility for those teaching composition to resist it:

> There is a political imperative to resist the privileging of individualism in this practice, for, as Terry Eagleton has demonstrated, it amounts to a form of coercion in the interests of conservative, elitist politics. (293)

The pedagogical alternative, composition as cultural studies, makes this process of social construction the center of the course. It invites students to see themselves as products of a culture and to resist the ready-made definitions, discourses, and "subject positions" that seem so "natural," so "normalized," so freely chosen. They begin to see all discourse as inevitably ideological, as "owned" and maintained by some group for very interested reasons. By gaining a critical awareness of these forms of language, the students gain a provisional freedom, they shed their "false consciousness." They look behind the screen and see who is pulling the strings.

Cause and Similarity

For a pragmatic argument, this one proceeds in an empirical vacuum. How do we evaluate the effect of one writing course on the political consciousness of students? Have expressivist pedagogies led to isolation, alienation, and an accommodation to the status quo? I've seen no evidence of this cause-and-effect relationship in my own teaching, and these critics provide none. The argument really rests not on any evidence of causation but on similarity. To paraphrase Berlin, there are attitudes and values fostered in expressionist pedagogies that *resemble* those that a capitalistic system seeks to foster in consumers (the self-gratifying enjoyment of "choice") and in entrepreneurs (private initiative). Because of this similarity, expressivist teaching causes students to enter happily and even successfully into that system.

This argument is so loose that it can easily be used against the cultural studies approach Berlin promotes. One could easily imagine how corporations could profit from the critical skills students develop when they "problemitize" seemingly self-evident arguments and positions. This training could produce a corps of troubleshooters who can penetrate the "normal" way of doing business so as to generate alternative and more profitable procedures. There *is* a resemblance. By the same token it is possible to argue that expressivism, with its emphasis on self-direction and personal uniqueness, can contribute to the exalted sense of agency that characterizes true social revolutionaries like Margaret Sanger.

Or it can be played another way. The cultural studies course *resembles* the traditional, teacher-directed classroom in several key ways. In most versions the reading material is chosen by the teacher, assignments are designed by the teacher, even the desired political orientation (leftist) is established by the teacher. In other words, this approach often seems to reestablish the hierarchical power relationship that expressivist pedagogies attempted to redefine. One might argue that whatever liberatory rationale that might be given for such a course, it *enacts* a politics very similar to the traditional teacher-directed classroom. To follow out this argument from similarity, this clear hierarchy may pave the way not for active citizenship but for submission to authority. In short, *because any two entities are similar in some way, there is virtually no restriction on the possible claims of causation that can be made.*

There are several other questions that this argument raises:

- How can teachers foster "resistance" to a capitalistic system that they themselves benefit from?

- How can expressivist pedagogy be accused of perpetuating "alienation" and "isolation" when it has pioneered ways of creating learning communities in the classroom?

- Exactly how does the genre or "subject position" students take on in forms like the eulogy, which predate capitalism, reinforce dominant capitalist ideology?

- If an openly stated goal of this approach is, as Bizzell (1991) states, to move students toward leftist political positions, why were proponents so shocked that they met opposition at the University of Texas?

- Lester Faigley (1992) seems to oppose the "institutional exercise of power" implicit in expressivist pedagogy (where students are rewarded for adopting certain "subjectivities"). Yet what is to prevent cultural studies from simply substituting one form of coercion for another, one preferred subjectivity for another? Isn't this an even greater danger in a pedagogy that has the stated goal of moving students toward politically preferable positions?

I want to focus on the construction of the student in these argument—and of the teacher's relationship to the students. Students are pictured as morally and civically deficient, though not through any real fault of their own. They are products of a media culture that has inculcated values in them that perpetuate consumption and rationalize social inequalities. Many of these values take the form of "commonplaces" that place the responsibility for social ills upon individuals acting as autonomous agents ("life is what you make it"). When students rely on these commonplaces in their writing, they are not simply using clichés, they are acting in bad faith. This state of development is similar to Kierkegaard's "despair of not knowing you are in despair," the sunny and dishonest optimism that he saw as a refusal to confront issues of faith and meaning. The instructor, aware of how these constructions work, operates on a higher moral plane and by calling these moralized beliefs into question, can create the critical awareness necessary for true resistance. One goal, according to France (1993), is for students to:

> Learn to shift rhetorical practices so that they not only can write personal, self-reflective essays and adept critiques of cultural texts, but can also assume a position critical of their culture's fondest truths. (606)

France singles out country music themes as ideal topics for this kind of critique.

There is a curious schizophrenia in this image of culture. This approach is based on the premise that we are culturally defined beings—sustained, gratified, and guided by the discourses around us. Yet the very cultural commonplaces, the moral bedrock embodied in these discourses, are quickly dismissed; Bartholomae and Petrosky (1986) claim that students using these cultural "truths" are simply appropriating the language of adult authority. There is no ethnographic interest in the moral utility of these commonplaces, or in the possibility that students may not be parroting the language of authority, but testifying to beliefs that have meant something in their lives. The fact that France singles out country music (as opposed to classical music) indicates the ease with which the preferences and pleasure of a social class (and region) can be dismissed. Cultural studies, as described by Berlin and France, is, at its root, distrustful of culture.

Because of its orientation toward political consciousness and civic action, cultural studies often dismisses pleasure and gratification as states of false consciousness induced by a media culture. Capitalism *sells* gratification —and students buy. Yet to turn these descriptions of pleasure into critiques denies the integrity of the gratifying experience. To treat rock music, for example, as a form of manipulation is to stand, uncomprehendingly, outside of the youth culture, a strange position for someone interested in cultural studies. Is it appropriate to turn to following description of a rock concert into a study of how the writer is "a product of culture"?

"Poke a double decker on a Llama; Taboot."

I turned back to the stage and began to dance again. My anklets jingled around my legs and my dress swirled around my body. I pressed the Poland Spring bottle cap into the palm of my hand and felt the ridges make an imprint on my flesh. I scraped my hand over the ridges and felt the sharp sensations run up my arm into my whole body.

"Llama, Taboot Taboot."

Every hair follicle was standing on end as my mane danced around my face and clung to my lips. It covered my face like a curtain and separated me from the rest of the world. I was dancing in my own realm. I watched my pink and purple sundress float around my legs. I grabbed some of it in my hands and felt the smooth cotton fabric with my fingers. I danced with the bottle cap in one hand and my dress clenched in the other.

The writer, in my view, has caught the sensuality of this moment; to suggest the "constructedness" of this experience would appear condescending and insensitive.

One strength of expressivist pedagogy is its endorsement of narrative pleasure. In Peter Elbow's terms, it provides a place for "rendering" (1990,

191); in Britton's scheme pleasure comes in the savoring of "form" that occurs in the spectator role: in Murray's version it is the pleasure of "surprise," of "expecting the unexpected," of seeming to follow the guidance of the language that evolves on the page. Reading can be a form of seduction described by Bill Buford, fiction editor for *The New Yorker*:

> Strong narrative writing is, at its most elementary, an act of seduction: its object is arousal. It arouses a curiosity, an interest, an expectation. It flirts with the reader, stimulates an appetite, verges on satisfying it, only to stimulate another, even greater appetite—an appetite for more, please, now. Is it really so strange that in the eighteenth century, novels were regarded as corrupting, and not the sort of thing a young woman should read on her own. Story means pleasure as distinct from art; it would rather gratify than edify. (1996, 12)

Expressivist pedagogy, while shying away from this explicit sexual metaphor, acknowledges that hedonism is a basic motivating force in language use. Advocates of cultural studies have far greater difficulty coming to terms with pleasure. The same could be said, generally, for the culture of the university as it drifts toward neo-Puritanism.

An Ethic of Care

The most persistent charge made against expressivism is that of "individualism"—the construction of self as isolated, solipsistic, focused on purely personal gratification and success, oblivious to the communal responsibility. Individualism equates with *selfishness*, indeed it seems to endorse it. Anyone who has invited personal autobiographical writing knows that some writing merits this charge—it seems private, not engaged with the world; the writer assumes little responsibility to engage seriously with the topic or the audience. I remember once I was frustrated with the reading responses of a graduate student that seemed only outpourings of frustration, anger, and occasionally agreement. She responded, "But that's how I feel." I asked her why a reader would be interested in this raw feeling. In other words, the "self" that she was expressing was one with no obligations or imperatives. All the writer must do is "reveal" the emotional state of this "self" and the reader, presumably, must accept it as "authentic." This corrupt, impoverished view of expressivism deserves to be rebuked.

Surprisingly absent from this critique of individualism is any reference to James Kinneavy's (1971) classic text, *A Theory of Discourse*, particularly his analysis of "the self that expresses." The self for Kinneavy is not a static entity that is "revealed." Drawing on the work of French existentialists and phenomenologists, he views the "self" as a set of conscious relationships, each with implicit moral responsibilities. The "self" is not something the individual "has"; it is more a freely chosen project: "we are, whether we like it or not, what we have made of ourselves in the past; finally we are what we are striving to be" (398). (Foucault and his followers would call this position "old duffer Humanism" [see Miller 1993, 43].)

One form of consciousness defined by Kinneavy is "Being for Others"; we become "selves" through the intersubjective process of engaging with others who give the individual status as "somebody." Echoing Martin Buber, Kinneavy claims that this "Being for Others" entails a moral obligation as well:

> I cannot achieve this added dimension of myself, however, if I treat the Other as only another object in the world. I must respect him as another consciousness, another subject. If I treat the Other as only another object, I lose my nature, I am no longer somebody. . . . (399)

In Buber's (1970) terms, I become a self when I am part of an "I-Thou" relationship; I lose that selfhood in an I-It relationship, when the other is simply an instrument for my own purposes.

Kinneavy is clearly working at a high level of abstraction, and I can't be sure that, as I look at student writing, I am doing justice to his formulation. Yet it does seem that in much of the personal writing that "works," the writer achieves this "Being for Others," what the authors of *Women's Ways of Knowing* (Belenky et al. 1986) have called "connected knowing," what Nell Noddings (1984) has called an "ethic of care." The writing is respectful, empathetic, and detailed enough to provide the sense of a fully human "other." It is writing that, in my view, has moral integrity and stands as evidence against "deficit" claims that the writers are simply "products" of a media culture.

Take, for example, Lori Quackenbush's unforgettable image of her grandfather moving into senility:

> I remember seeing a small dog jump from the bed of a pick-up truck as it stopped for a red light. When the light changed the truck pulled away, heading down the road. The dog in sudden panic, ran after it. Faster than I'd ever seen a dog run. But the truck gained speed and left the animal farther and farther behind. He kept running till I could no longer see him, his fear pushing him down the road.
>
> I felt that way when my grandfather started to die. His age was carrying him away, faster and faster and no matter how I ran I couldn't catch him, couldn't make him stop.

Another theme that shows the ethical sensibility of students is work, particularly the way oppressive supervisors and dulling routines dehumanize the worker. With more students than ever working, this is a topic I want to invite, sometimes with an excerpt from Studs Terkel's *Working,* sometimes with papers like Joanna Lucy's "All in a Day's Work." Using a clipped present tense style, she takes us through her father's day as a motel manager:

> The alarm clock goes off. It is 6 A.M.; time to get up. My father has not slept all night. His paranoia about something terrible happening to the motel while he is sleeping keeps him awake. He rolls out of bed and makes his way into the bathroom to get ready for a new day of aggravation.
>
> He goes to the bathroom. He climbs into the shower for five minutes, anything longer is just wasting water. In this day and age, no one can afford to waste anything. . . .

Business is bad this summer.

> Each day he looks back a year or two [in his log] for preparation and comparison. This year has been the worst of all twenty-seven years in business. Looking back only makes the sting worse. He looks anyway.

The day proceeds—he helps clean rooms, makes a trip to the bank, recites his monologue for guests ("This is the lobby; brochures on the back wall . . ."), and drinks a screwdriver at 3:30. The day drags on:

> Cars come and go; some he loses; some he does not want; some are just turning around. He is on the phone almost constantly to other motel owners and businessmen discussing business and aggravating each other. He has a few more drinks, waits, watches, and prays.
>
> Regardless of how good or bad business is, when dinner rolls around, the cars roll in. Rarely my father eats a meal still hot. Customers do not hesitate to interrupt our meals, or anything else. There is little privacy when you are running a motel. There is, also, little relaxation, and this summer, little business. It is no wonder my father has high blood pressure, drinks, and is a nervous wreck.
>
> After dinner, he reclines in his chair to watch the news. Cars come and cars go. The phone rings constantly. By 8:30 Dad's falling asleep in his chair, so he drags himself up, shuts off the post and porch lights, and goes to bed. His day is done. He will awake tomorrow to continue the interminable cycle of drudgery.

Joanna is able to re-create the tedium and constant anxiety of her father's work. Her syntax, stripped of elaboration and any richness, mirrors the consecutive, dulling tasks her father must perform. Rhetoricians sometimes refer to this quality as "presence," the need for the writer to make vivid a present moment because, as Francis Bacon wrote, "the affection beholdeth merely the present" (Perelman and Olbrechts-Tyteca 1969, 117).

The capacity is well-demonstrated in the essay by Jill Daly (1994), "Simply Chris," which has become a classic in the Boston College writing program. Daly describes the autism of her adopted younger brother and the ways in which his defenses are easily overwhelmed by sensory stimuli:

> There are times when Christopher does not have a chance to put up this protective wall. I came home one evening with a group of friends, all of whom were strangers to Chris. He was sitting on the rocking chair in the living room, watching a video of NBA Super Slams, part of the bedroom routine. My friends and I entered the room, and said "hello" to him. Suddenly every muscle in his body became a rock. He was straining to keep focusing on the television, on the ball in the hands of the player in the video, but he couldn't ignore faces, voices, and bodies that were surrounding him in the room. The walls were closing in. I could see the tears welling up in his eyes and the amount of force he was exerting while trying to hold them back. And then he let go. He gave up, and the tears began to flow like water from a dam that had just been broken. He fled from the room, screaming, and collapsed in our mother's arms.

Daly's paper is a profound act of human curiosity, and ultimately empathy. The very act of identification serves as a moral impulse for the writer, who at the time of the writing volunteered at a home for autistic children; it also takes the reader inside a "present" moment so that we begin to experience the panic of an autistic child when his fragile sensory protection is overwhelmed. Daly's great achievement is not that she abstracts from personal experience— but that she *penetrates* it.

Extending Boundaries/Endorsing Boundaries

The boundary to what is possible in writing is a fiction created by and within writing. Only when the boundary is recognized as moveable can it be a regenerative element in art, rather than an obstacle to its growth.

—William Davidson

Although I have tried to defend autobiographical writing against the criticisms of cultural studies advocates, it is clear that I share some of their assumptions. The student who writes personally is not revealing a unique self—if that were the case it would be pointless to generalize about it. We would be at a conceptual dead end. It is far more profitable to view students as occupying subject positions, trying on "subjectivities" that are made available in a literate culture. Sentimental literature, pastoral literature, confessional literature—all part of the available repertoire. Furthermore each tradition predisposes the writer to see some things and miss others. Finally, to be aware of these traditions *as traditions,* and not "natural" ways of self-representation, can increase options by allowing us to see boundaries as "moveable." This is the core of agreement.

The disagreement centers on one major issue. Cultural studies, as depicted by major figures in the field of composition, takes a defensive attitude toward culture. Discourse co-opts us, manipulates us, provides ready-made categories that very likely serve the interests of others. Resistance and critique become the only uncorrupted discourse forms, the only form of writing that can keep us from being "written" by our culture. This seems to me an entirely too austere, and monolithic, view of culture. Discourse forms can also invite us to take on roles of moral seriousness. We wear a mask, notes Robert Park (1950), often one that epitomizes a cultural and ethical ideal:

> In a sense, and in so far as the mask represents the conception we have formed of ourselves—the role we are striving to live up to—this mask is our truer self, the self we would like to be. (249)

The subject position that Joanna Lucy takes in "All in a Day's Work" is not one she invented. The daughter-concerned-for-the-physical-and-mental-(and spiritual)-deterioration-of-her-father is a cultural position, an established moral position (and not one without dangers). It is one which invites the writer to take on a moral seriousness, to "live up to" an ethical version of herself.

In claiming that a culture offers a repertoire of subject positions, I do not want to minimize the postmodern imperative to challenge the boundaries of these positions (though this is a trail I have not followed in this book). We can see such a challenge in the writing of Victor Vitanza, the collaborative texts Lad Tobin and Lester Faigley describe, and the multigenre papers of Tom Romano. Paradoxically, leftist cultural studies, which rests on postmodern theories, has been very conservative in the formal options it offers students. We see very little of the irreverence, play, improvisation, and humor so evident in postmodern writing. In fact, we see little student writing at all in many of these descriptions; students are virtually absent in Berlin's final book, *Rhetorics, Poetics, and Cultures* (1996). One would expect invitations for students to play with multivoiced texts, to innovate structurally so that the eye does not move in straight linear fashion line-to-line-to-line. One would expect visual experimentation, what Blake (1995) called "visionary forms dramatic" instead of "cold print and type."

I suspect two factors hold cultural studies back. One is the political mission of developing a leftist political consciousness in students; given this aim, much avant-garde literature would seem to have little political utility. The other factor is the close alliance of cultural studies, despite its radicalism, to traditional academic forms. The writing cultural studies advocates is itself clearly within the genres of academic argumentation (and remote from the literary experimentation going on). The pedagogy seems to reproduce a discourse that is academically respectable.

But "academic discourse," the focus of so much attention in our field, is a slow-moving train; it is doubtful it can be very sympathetic to Blake's (1995) injunction, used to open a recent collection of postmodern poetry:

> Obey Thou the Words of the Inspired Man
> All that can be annihilated must be annihilated.

A few months ago I attended a talk given by Helen Fox Mazer, a prolific writer of adolescent fiction (as is her husband). She told the story of how they began to write for publication. They had been talking for years about giving up their jobs and doing what they loved to do, but they couldn't find the money to buy the window of time to begin. Then Helen injured her neck in a car crash, and with the insurance money they realized they could have three months. They quit their jobs, held family expenses to a minimum, wrote every morning, began to sell some magazine pieces, and never looked back.

Three months, I thought, earned the hard way, through a whiplashed neck. Though she tried to downplay any sense of hardship, it seemed to me a powerful act of self-direction. I had wasted more time than that in aimless reading and general paralysis, what I hoped was some form of rehearsal for writing this book. And my neck was fine.

Mazer's story, like many of the testimonies of writers, was an enabling one, though it boils down to a piece of folk wisdom. Life is what you make it. In reduced form we can recognize Mazer's message as that commonplace—a "life lesson," the success story of the self-made man, or in this case, couple. Surely we now know that this freedom to create ourselves, to choose our future, is highly constrained, that we are "products of a culture," that this very myth is an American product. And yet . . . when my mother was twenty, teaching high school and discouraged, she remembers waiting for a bus in Tiffin, Ohio. A lawyer in the town stood beside her, saw her mood, and said, seemingly out of the blue, "Make yourself the master of every situation." She never saw him again. But over sixty years later she remembers this advice as a serendipitous act of kindness.

It may be time to admit the obvious, that expressivist pedagogy *is* romantic, that romanticism is deeply embedded in American literary traditions (and I would wager into the actual belief system of even its critics). This romanticism has extraordinary resonance with young writers. It is empowering for students—for all of us—to believe:

- that we can imagine ourselves as coherent selves with coherent histories and can therefore create stories about ourselves
- that this coherence, this "identity," allows for a sense of agency, a trajectory into the future
- that we each see the world in a distinctive way and have the ability to make a distinctive contribution to it
- that human beings share an essence that allows the "I" of the writer to become a mirror for us all
- that knowing entails feeling, and that discourse becomes sterile if it shuts out emotion
- that openness to the particularity of the natural world, what Lawrence Buell calls an "environmental imagination" serves as a check to human egotism and can create a sense of stewardship.

It is empowering to believe that language can apprehend experience, that it can render in William Carlos William's (1968) words "a new world naked," that it is not a series of deferrals. Charles Simic (1994) writes:

> The secret wish of poetry is to stop time. The poet wants to retrieve a face, a mood, a cloud in the sky, a tree in the wind, and make a kind of mental photograph of that moment in which you as a reader recognize yourself. (2)

Later, he quotes Octavio Paz:

> "To unlock the instant, to/ penetrate its astonished rooms . . ." Here's a point at which time and eternity, history and consciousness meet, a fragment of time haunted by the whole of time. The present is the only place where we experience the eternal. The eternal shrinks to the size of the present because only the present can be humanly grasped. (56)

This belief, then, is part of the mythos of a major American literary tradition; it survives because it has proven itself pragmatically as a generative description of perception. That our language falls short of this ideal is inevitable. As

Flaubert wrote, "Human speech is like a cracked kettle on which we tap crude rhythms for bears to dance to, while we long to make music that will melt the stars." And often even the bears don't dance.

Yet the testimonies of writers that Don Murray and others have collected take us inside the lore of writers, acquaint us with a generative set of sometimes contradictory beliefs and habits. It may be that these self-descriptions are inaccurate, that they leave a lot out, that they contain a bit of posturing—yet they speak to beginning writers and others for whom the achievement of "self" is more than a theoretical issue.

8

Final Stories
(Each with a Moral)

I do not believe that an old man's pessimism is necessarily truer than a young man's optimism simply because it comes after. There are things a young man knows that are true and are not yet in the old man's power to recollect.

—Richard Rodriguez, "Late Victorians"

Postmodernism—Must I Belong to This Club?

Every Friday night in the summer, the air in Durham is filled with a hum, something like the sound of an annoying insect, a big one like a circling horsefly. The sound rises and falls as the super-modified racing cars circle the one-third mile track of the Lee Speedway in an astonishing seven seconds, accelerating to 130 miles per hour on the short straightaways. When these cars race attendance sometimes reach about 6,000—more than the typical University of New Hampshire football game.

When I was a kid I heard the sound of car races that filtered in from the dirt track of the County Fairgrounds—though our family rarely went. The kids in the neighborhood bought small plastic cars that we raced, soapbox-derby style, along the sidewalk in front of our house. Each car had a number corresponding to one of the fairground's stock car driver, and we kept records for distance.

Attending these races is a working-class pleasure, one that I've renewed over the past few years. When I mention to university colleagues that I love to go they look at me puzzled and ask, "But isn't it loud?" And I answer, "Yes, *that's the point.*" You feel your body invaded by sound; you feel the sound in your head, your heart, your lungs, your skin. It is extreme, on the edge of tolerance. I make no converts, and I suspect that Bourdieu would explain that this disapproval of car racing is an element of the "taste" that a college education seeks to foster. Imagine a student who wanted to do his research paper on Richard Petty.

Nowhere is the class-bound division more evident than in the frequent assertion by academicians that we live in a "postmodern age," one in which foundational beliefs in rationality and "essences" are discredited. Often there is something mildly coercive in these assertions; as if the issue has been settled, the paradigm shifted. In academic debate, merely to use the label "essentialist" is often enough to discredit an idea. Yet at the same time the "postmodern era" is being proclaimed, surveys show that an increasing majority of Americans claim to be religious, believing in a Supreme Being who transcends history and culture. I would guess an even larger majority would claim that some values— "self-evident" truths such as human equality—are enduringly and essentially true, not simply "constructs" of a particular culture at a particular historical moment. It is paradoxical, if not hypocritical, for compositionists to argue for the centrality of "class" in our understanding of students, and at the same time advocate a form of skepticism that is antipathetic to the sources of moral and spiritual power in many working-class communities.

In the composition classroom, there are also favored modes of moral self-presentation. In one the writer presents herself as *in process,* moving from less to more enlightened (more complex and individuated) stages of aware-ness. As shown in Chapter 2, the hinge of change is the significant event, the turn, that the writer represents and draws meaning from. Morality is a form of growth, and the writer comes to write about these earlier "selves" with detachment, almost as if she were writing about a different person.

In contrast, the working class represented by Shirley Heath (1983) in *Ways with Words* would see morality not as growth but a form of steadfastness, of not straying from a set of basic rules of behavior. Complexity, subtlety— even education—may serve to distract attention from core values and proper modes of action. This pietistic view of morality pervades Biblical teaching. In Micah, for example, the proper spiritual stance is described succinctly:

> He hath showed thee, O man, what is good; and what doth the Lord require of thee, but to do justly, and to love mercy, and to walk humbly with thy God? (Micah 6:8)

The "but" in this injunction is significant. The demands are not conceptually complex, yet they require what Robert Coles calls moral and spiritual "stam-ina" to overcome human egotism that causes us to lose sight of them. Trans-lated into student writing, this view of morality can seem static, conventional, commonsensical, and unreflective. Since the most powerful statements of moral behavior exist *prior* to the writing, the narrative serves to exemplify that truth. It is unlikely, indeed egotistical, to think something new would emerge.

Students of moral development like Lawrence Kohlberg (1972) place this kind of thinking at a "pre-conventional" or "pre-moral" level because there is not the complex decision making that is a central characteristic of "principled morality." Not incidentally he found this capacity develops faster in middle-class students. I wonder how "principled," in this sense, my grandfather would turn out. Would his unbendable code of putting others first appear premoral?

To put the matter another way, there may be a confusion here between aesthetics and morality. Clearly there are forms of self-presentation that seem more pleasing, more attractive. They may be more elaborated, discursive, playful, skeptical; they create a sense of openness, of a mind moving toward understanding, provisional as it might be. The "self" that appears to operate on unshakable first principals seems more wooden, inflexible, less attractive. Yet from a moral standpoint—and there is, of course, a tendency to claim moral weight for versions of literacy—this preference seems to break down. In a crisis it is often this wholeheartedness, this unshakableness, that we rely upon.

I am not, however, making an argument for passivity, complete acceptance, or paralysis. The fact that some of students may prefer forms of self-presentation that conflict with the norms of an English department writing culture does not mean we can't teach those norms. We *can* raise questions about accepted belief, work to complicate student understandings, push them to understand alternative positions. We can create what Donna Qualley (1997) calls a "counter-discourse" that invites a more complex alternative. Yet the spirit of this invitation is critical. It is one thing to demonstrate an alternative—to extend a repertoire; it is another to try to eradicate a "lower" form of consciousness.

Mike Rose (1989) relates an incident in *Lives on the Boundary* that illustrates this attitude. In one of his varied teaching assignments, he taught poetry, via telephone, to residents of convalescent homes and shut-ins throughout Los Angeles County. The poems Rose selected were short, direct, and imagistic. After a while some of the participants began cutting out poems they liked and reading them to Rose, poems like this:

> Will she ever come to my castle of dreams—
> To those gardens of rarest bloom?
> Will she ever see the sparkling streams
> Where gentle lights illume?

The poems were sentimental, archaic, "they were the kinds of poems all my schooling had trained me to dismiss."

He rehearses some critical reactions, none of which feel right. Then, in talking to his mother he has an insight:

My mother called me one night to ask me if I thought a card she bought for the doctor was okay. She read me the Hallmark rhyme and I was about the tell her what I thought when it hit me. Addie and Ernest and the rest weren't sending me poems for criticism; they wanted to pass on a gift or show off a little—they wanted to participate in some fuller way. (163)

Rose ended up xeroxing the poems he chose alongside those chosen by his students—the participants ended up liking both kinds.

There is the related question of how we deal with "wholehearted" discourse, writing that portrays relationships and experience in unqualified, unambivalent terms—the testimonial, the tribute, the eulogy. It is tempting, though I think beyond a certain point unproductive, to adopt the "worm-in-the-apple" attitude: since all relationships are complex and conflictual any writing that pretends to uncomplicated admiration or happiness is essentially self-deceptive. John Cheever (1980) satirizes this attitude in his short story, "The Worm in the Apple":

> The Crutchmans were so very, very happy and so temperate in all their habits and so pleased with everything that came their way that one was bound to suspect a worm in their rosy apple and that the extraordinary rosiness of the fruit was only meant to conceal the gravity and depth of the infection. (338)

It was this very worm I was looking for when I asked Alan (see Chapter 4) to search for flaws in his state-champion wrestler brother. I wonder now if it is not better to work within these genres: to accept the lack of ambivalence and help the writer make them stronger, more convincing tributes—and at the same time to show portraits, such as Steinem's "Ruth's Song," that shows a more complex relationship. As Rose discovered, there may be a place for both.

Where Have the Writers Gone?

When I gave my job talk at the University of New Hampshire in 1977, I was introduced as a "composition expert" by the chair of the department, who himself was a Pulitzer Prize winner. In the audience, listening to this composition expert were a National Book Award Winner, a finalist for that award, and a poet who would go on to win a McArthur Grant and the Pulitzer Prize. Fraudulence barely described the sense of inadequacy I felt.

The obvious problem for me, and for the "field" of composition, was to establish some sort of authority in the presence of professional writers. What could I add to the knowledge of craft they had accumulated? Why shouldn't professional writers be the ones to take control of all of the writing courses?

(Only later did I realize most of them wouldn't be caught dead near a Freshman English class.) Donald Murray (1968), the Pulitzer Prize winner in the crowd, had written in *A Writer Teaches Writing* that professional writers should be the exemplars from whom we might learn about the processes, attitudes, and craft. Those in composition might study what writers did and translate it into teaching strategies.

Murray's truly subversive move in all this was not to advocate that writing was a process (what *isn't* a process?), but to claim that the professional writer (and not the academician) should be the model for the student. This *public* form of writing should be at the center of the course. And though Murray claims that the memo-writer is as much a writer as the poet, he clearly make a special place for creative writers whom he quotes with great regularity. So even though a composition course may be required by the university, writing is not defined by the academic expectations of the university.

This may seem a bit of arcane history, but I want to argue that the alliance of composition to creative writing is essential for creating space for personal writing. The classics of expressivism, Macrorie's (1970) *Telling Writing*, for example, is actually a very practical guide to the craft of literary fiction and nonfiction with its chapters on creating tension, telling details, the use of dialogue.

But Murray's prescription for the research role of composition was disciplinary poison. Those in composition were not themselves "writers," yet they would study those who were so that they might help create conditions in the classroom to enable students to experience the act of writing as performed by professionals. The obvious question is: why not let writers themselves run the show? Do we need a class of professionals simply to study and translate the processes of creative writers?

The divorce between writing and composition is one of the great unexamined stories in English studies. Illogical in one sense, it was a professional necessity on the other. As Steve North (1987) has pointed out, a precondition for becoming a "field" is demonstrating the inadequacy of the practitioner lore. And while he refers specifically to teaching lore, his point is relevant to that of writers. If this lore (e.g., the interviews in the *Paris Review*, William Stafford's "A Way of Writing," Annie Dillard's *Teaching a Stone to Talk*) were sufficient, there would be no need for another, more systematic, form of knowledge-creation.

The divorce takes many forms. There is the shift of interest to academic writing in the mid eighties, a move that not incidentally coincides with emergence of a generation of academically trained composition specialists. This shift has the double benefit of administrative approval for taking university writing (and not popular writing) as the guide for developing a writing program. It also, finally, allows the compositionist to claim expertise in the kind of writing students are asked to do.

There is also the marginalization of creative writing, which plays little official part in the training of this new corps of composition professionals. Few programs (that I know of) require any evidence of proficiency in poetry, fiction, or the nonacademic essay as a condition of admission. The graduate program of study may include literary theory, but it is unlikely to involve graduate-level writing courses. Should composition students still maintain a private interest in poetry or fiction writing it is often best to keep that fact off the job application, lest someone on the search committee think that the candidate's true interest is writing and not composition.

If publishing is required, the reward system will favor the type of writing that most resembles academic scholarship in the English department. It is as if to prove itself composition must show it can quote French theorists too (as I have done here). The result is an inbred form of obscurity, and a distancing of "composition studies" from the practical realities of those who bear the brunt of composition teaching (those teaching in community college, for example), and not coincidentally, from those outside the mainstream of postsecondary education. It results in a neglect of writing issues in the public schools, something that could not be said about the first generation of composition scholars. And it, of course, increases the distance between writers and the field of composition.

Finally, the composition course itself begins to be shaped around a series of thematic readings, often dealing with issues of race or cultural difference. Though the rationale for this reading focus may be liberatory, the courses themselves often begin to take on a more traditional look (Tobin 1995b). It becomes harder for the student writing to be the "content" of the course; instead this writing explicates the reading. Cultural readings have replaced the literary readings that might have dominated the course in the early sixties, yet the look is familiar; in fact, it is the structure compositionists like Murray so strongly opposed.

Clearing the Apparatus

If one of the aims of a composition course is to make room for the representation and discussion of diversity, it follows that the invitation to write should be an open one. The more space the apparatus of the course takes up, the harder it is going to be to elicit this representation. I learned this lesson the hard way in my first semester of teaching. We had marched through the standard syllabus of the University of Texas, circa 1977, with its careful path through the modes of discourse, working toward a culminating paper, as I recall, in evaluation. Near the end of the course I was talking with a student about his work, and it became clear that he didn't have a clue about the differences between the assignment; I tried to explain, he tried to listen, but then just smiled, "What does it matter?"

I jettisoned the syllabus for the last assignment. I cleared the apparatus from the floor and asked them to write about something that mattered to them, meeting with each to talk about topics. I remember in particular an African American student from Sherman, Texas, who mentioned that he was one of twenty-eight brothers and sisters. In fourteen weeks of teaching I had managed *not* to learn this piece of information. He said he would have no trouble coming up with something to write about—and indeed, his paper on the shooting death of one of his brothers was powerful and heartbreaking. But it was the last one I saw. It left me wondering what more I could have learned. What was it like to live in a family of thirty people? What price, what sacrifices did it take to make his way from Sherman to Austin?

Diversity implies teacher ignorance. We need to learn about culture from the stories students tell. I remember another student in that Texas class, silent and invisible until the end, when she wrote passionately about how Mexican American students were tracked in the Brownsville schools (she was one of them). She was teaching me something about culture, and without the open space I had created I don't think I would have had the chance to learn it.

Lad Tobin (1995a), director of the First-Year Writing Program at Boston College, makes a useful analogy. He views the writing course as an open space, a "common," that needs to be protected from appropriation by academic disciplines such as cultural studies and literary studies. Rather than being a course focusing on "the language of the academy" it can be a place where writing is more broadly conceived, where students for one semester in their academic lives can try something different.

Of course there can be no truly open spaces. Language is irretrievably social, saturated with ownership, hierarchy, connotation, and prejudice. This situation troubled romantics like Rousseau, who at one point hoped he could discover a "language of things," a language not imbued with the weight of convention (and with the discovery of hieroglyphics he thought he might have found it). Even as students tell stories of their lives they operate within conventions of self-representation that I have explored in this book. Critics of expressivism have argued that those who claim to offer an "open space" are every bit as ideological, every bit as restrictive, as teachers who are more direct about their ideological beliefs; in fact, it is more honest to be explicit about authority than to keep it covert.

Yet there are degrees of freedom. The teacher who announces, as one of the teaching assistants at UNH once did, that he is "antifraternity" effectively reduces the range of positions a writer can take (students will prudently extrapolate from that position to others). The teacher who claims that all knowledge is "socially constructed" may silence the devout student who can find no way to speak of religious belief. The territory is reduced as students perceive a political orthodoxy, of the Left or Right, that writing must adhere to.

The ideological space of a composition course, while never unbounded, can be expanded or contracted—and students look to determine these degrees of freedom. Teachers who choose to keep this space relatively open are often perceived as being "soft," teaching "low risk" courses, not academically rigorous. Yet if we are to take culture seriously, if we are to learn about culture from our students, it follows that we need a space big enough for a diversity of forms of self-representation.

I finished most of this book before the fall of 1996, when I once again taught a section of Freshman English. At the time I realized that I didn't have an ending, nothing that said enough about what the "cash value" of the book would be for teachers. In my darker moments I wondered if the net effect of the book would only be to make a complicated job even more complicated. How, after all, could we rationalize our preferences if they do not represent "good writing" in any fundamental sense? No wonder cultures "normalize" values, make them appear self-evident, disguise their constructedness. No wonder they attach moral value to literary preferences. At least in that way the cognitive strain is eased. Is it in fact possible to honor multiple aesthetics?

But as I began to teach, I found that the analysis did help resolve a central tension I had felt for years. Previously I often felt constrained to dislike elements in student writing that I thoroughly approved in their lives—their optimism, energy, capacity for enjoyment, idealism. Translated into writing these qualities often appeared clichéd, trite, naïve; they were everything I had been conditioned to dislike. Like Hemingway's protagonist I felt obligated to be nauseated by this wholeheartedness. I would normally try to hide this nausea by ignoring what seemed like platitudes and focusing on something else in the writing.

This last semester, I tried to listen more carefully to these sections I had dismissed. A student writes about working in an animal shelter and concludes with her resolute conviction that she can make a difference for animals. I listen to that language of resolution and make a point of telling her how much I admire her conviction, her undeflectable self-confidence that would surface in several of her papers. It felt right. It felt as if I was finally paying attention.

And if that attitude seems "sentimental," it may be time to reexamine this term of rebuke.

Works Cited

Aristotle. [338 B.C.E.] 1991. *On Rhetoric: A Theory of Civic Discourse.* Translated by George Kennedy. New York: Oxford University Press.

Baldwin, James. [1955] 1984. "Notes of a Native Son." In *The Contemporary Essay,* edited by Donald Hall. New York: St. Martin's.

Bartholomae, David. 1985. "Inventing the University." In *When a Writer Can't Write,* edited by Mike Rose. New York: Guilford.

Bartholomae, David, and Anthony Petrosky. 1986. *Facts, Artifacts, and Counterfacts: Theory and Method for a Reading and Writing Course.* Portsmouth, NH: Boynton Cook/Heinemann.

Bauer, Dale. 1990. "The Other 'F' Word: Feminist in the Classroom." *College English* 52 (April): 385–96.

Baym, Nina. 1985. "Melodramas of Beset Manhood: How Theories of American Fiction Exclude Women Authors." From *The New Feminist Criticism: Essays on Women, Literature, and Theory,* edited by Elaine Schowalter. New York: Pantheon.

Belenky, Mary, et al. 1986. *Women's Ways of Knowing: The Development of Self, Voice, and Mind.* New York: Basic Books.

Berlin, James. 1996. *Rhetorics, Poetics, and Cultures: Refiguring English Studies.* Urbana, IL: National Council of Teachers of English.

———. 1988. "Rhetoric and Ideology in the Writing Class." *College English* 50 (5): 477–94.

Bizzell, Patricia. 1991. "Power, Authority, and Critical Pedagogy." *Journal of Basic Writing* 10 (2): 54–72.

Blake, William. 1995. "Obey Thou the Words of the Inspired Man." From *Milton: Book the Second.* In *Poems for the Millenium,* edited by Jerome Rothenberg and Pierre Joris. Volume 1. Berkeley: University of California Press.

Bleich, David. 1990. "Literacy and Citizenship: Resisting Social Issues." In *The Right to Literacy,* edited by Andrea Lunsford, Helen Moglen, and James Slevin. New York: Modern Language Association and the

National Council of Teachers of English.

Booth, Wayne. 1961. *The Rhetoric of Fiction.* Chicago: University of Chicago Press.

Bourdieu, Pierre. 1984. *Distinction: A Social Critique of Judgment and Taste.* Translated by Richard Nice. Cambridge: Harvard University Press.

Britton, James. 1970. *Language and Learning.* Miami: University of Miami Press.

Britton, James, et al. 1975. *The Development of Writing Abilities, 11–18.* London: Macmillan.

Buber, Martin. 1970. *I and Thou.* New York: Scribners.

Buell, Lawrence. 1995. *The Environmental Imagination: Thoreau, Nature Writing, and the Formation of American Culture.* Cambridge: Harvard University Press.

Buford, Bill. 1996. "The Seductions of Storytelling." *The New Yorker* (June 24/July 1): 11–12.

Camirand, Meghan. 1995. "My Father's Mother." In *Voices: University of New Hampshire Undergraduate English Journal 1994–5,* edited by Tamara Niedzolski.

Camus, Albert. 1942, 1946. *The Stranger.* Edited by Stuart Gilbert. New York: Vintage.

Cheever, John. 1980. *The Stories of John Cheever.* New York: Ballantine.

Chekhov, Anton. 1973. *Letters of Anton Chekhov.* Edited by Avrahm Yarmolinsky. New York: Viking.

Coles, Robert. 1986. *The Moral Lives of Children.* Boston: Houghton Mifflin.

Coles, William E., and James Vopat. 1985. *What Makes Writing Good: A Multiperspective.* Lexington, MA: D.C. Heath.

Connors, Robert. 1996. "Teaching and Learning as a Man." *College English 58* (2): 137–57.

———. 1994. "Static Abstractions." In *The Writing Teacher's Sourcebook,* edited by Edward Corbett and Gary Tate. New York: Oxford University Press.

Conrad, Joseph. [1903] 1966. "Youth." In *Great Short Works of Joseph Conrad.* New York: Harper and Row.

Cooper, Charles, and Lee Odell. 1977. *Evaluating Writing: Describing, Measuring, Judging.* Urbana, IL: National Council of Teachers of English.

Corbett, Edward P. J. 1971. *Classical Rhetoric for the Modern Student.* 2d ed. New York: Oxford University Press.

Daly, Jill Eileen. 1994. "Simply Chris." In *Fresh Ink: Essays from Boston College's First-Year Writing Program, 1993–1994,* edited by Eileen Donovan and Lad Tobin. Chestnut Hill: Boston College.

Didion, Joan. 1979. *The White Album.* New York: Farrar, Straus & Giroux.

Diederich, Paul. 1974. *Measuring Growth in English.* Champaign, IL: National Council of Teachers of English.

Dillard, Annie. 1982. *Teaching a Stone to Talk: Expeditions and Encounters.* New York: Harper and Row.

DiPentima, Matthew. 1994. "Frankie's Drive-In." In *Fresh Ink: Essays from Boston College's First-Year Writing Program, 1993–1994,* edited by Eileen Donovan and Lad Tobin. Chestnut Hill: Boston College.

Dixon, John, and Leslie Stratta. 1986. *Writing Narrative—and Beyond.* Ottawa: Canadian Council of Teachers of English.

Dostoievsky, Feodor. [1865] 1950. *The Brothers Karamazov.* Translated by Constance Garnett. New York: Grosset and Dunlap.

Eagleton, Terry. 1983. *Literary Theory.* Minneapolis: University of Minnesota Press.

Elbow, Peter. 1990. *What Is English?* Urbana, IL: National Council of Teachers of English.

———. 1973. *Writing Without Teachers.* New York: Oxford University Press.

Eliot, T. S. 1950. *Selected Essays.* New York: Harcourt Brace.

Erickson, Erik. 1968. *Identity: Youth and Crisis.* New York: Norton.

Faigley, Lester. 1992. *Fragments of Rationality: Postmodernity and the Subject of Composition.* Pittsburgh: University of Pittsburgh Press.

France, Alan. 1993. "Assigning Places: The Function of Introductory Composition as a Cultural Discourse." *College English* 55 (6): 593–609.

Gleick, James. 1992. *Genius: The Life and Science of Richard Feynman.* New York: Pantheon.

Goffman, Erving. 1959. *The Presentation of Self in Everyday Life.* New York: Anchor Books.

Hairston, Maxine. 1992. "Diversity, Ideology, and Teaching Writing." *College Composition and Communication* 43 (2): 479–93.

Harris, Joseph. 1987. "The Plural Text/The Plural Self: Roland Barthes and William Coles." *College English* 49: 158–70.

Havelock, Eric. 1963. *Preface to Plato.* Cambridge: Harvard University Press.

Heaney, Seamus. 1980. *Poems 1965–1975.* New York: Farrar, Straus & Giroux.

Heath, Shirley Brice. 1983. *Ways with Words: Language, Life, and Work in Communities and Classrooms.* Cambridge, England: Cambridge University Press.

Hemingway, Ernest. 1938. "Soldier's Home." In *The Short Stories of Ernest Hemingway,* 143–54. New York: Scribners.

Hill, Adams Sherman. 1896. *The Foundations of Rhetoric.* New York: Harpers.

Holy Bible, King James Version. Cleveland and New York: The World Publishing Company.

James, William. [1896] 1948. "The Will to Believe." In *Essays in Pragmatism,* edited by Alburey Castell, 88–109. New York: Hafner Press.

———. 1902. *The Varieties of Religious Experience: A Study in Human Nature.* New York: The Modern Library.

———. 1960. *The Selected Letters of William James,* edited by Elizabeth Hardwick. New York: Farrar, Straus and Cudahy.

Johnson, Samuel. [1752] 1969. "No. 196." *The Yale Edition of the Works of Samuel Johnson,* Volume 5, The Rambler, edited by W. J. Bate and Albrecht B. Straus, 257–261.

Joyce, James. [1916] 1964. *A Portrait of the Artist as a Young Man.* New York: Viking.

Kinneavy, James L. 1971. *A Theory of Discourse.* Englewood Cliffs, NJ: Prentice-Hall.

Knoblauch, C. H., and Lil Brannon. 1984. *Rhetorical Traditions and the Teaching of Writing.* Portsmouth, NH: Boynton Cook/Heinemann.

Kohlberg, Lawrence. 1972. "A Cognitive-Developmental Approach to Moral Development." *Humanist* (November–December): 13–16.

Langer, Judith. 1995. *Envisioning Literature: Literary Understanding and Literature Instruction.* New York: Teachers College Press.

Leopold, Aldo. [1949] 1968. *A Sand County Almanac.* New York: Oxford University Press.

Levine, David. 1995. Commencement address, University of New Hampshire, Durham, NH.

Li, Xiao-ming. 1996. *"Good Writing" in Cross Cultural Context.* Albany: State University of New York Press.

Lopate, Phillip. 1994. Introduction to *The Art of the Personal Essay.* New York: Anchor.

Macrorie, Ken. 1970. *Telling Writing.* 2d ed. Rochelle Park, New Jersey: Hayden.

Marback, Richard. 1996. "Corbett's Hand: A Rhetorical Figure for Composition Studies." *College Composition and Communication* 47 (2): 180–98.

Mencken, H. L. [1926] 1977. "The Last New Englander." In *Prejudices: Fifth Series,* pp. 244–54. New York: Octagon Books.

Miller, James. 1993. *The Passion of Michel Foucault.* New York: Anchor.

Miller, Susan. 1990. *Textual Carnivals: The Politics of Composition.* Carbondale, IL: Southern Illinois University Press.

Mitchell, Joseph. 1993. *Up in the Old Hotel.* New York: Vintage.

Montaigne, Michel de. [1580] 1957. *The Complete Works of Montaigne.* Translated by Donald Frame. Stanford: Stanford University Press.

Murray, Donald. 1996. *Crafting a Life: In Essay, Story, Poem.* Portsmouth, NH: Boynton Cook/Heinemann.

———. 1989. *Expecting the Unexpected: Teaching Myself and Others to Read and Write*. Portsmouth, NH: Boynton Cook/Heinemann.

———. 1968. *A Writer Teaches Writing: A Practical Method of Teaching Composition*. Boston: Houghton Mifflin.

New York Times. 1988. Transcript of the Presidential Debate, October 14, A-14.

Newkirk, Thomas. 1994. "The Politics of Intimacy: Barrett Wendell's Defeat at Harvard." In *Taking Stock: The Writing Process Movement in the 90s*, edited by Lad Tobin and Thomas Newkirk, 115–32. Portsmouth, NH: Boynton Cook/Heinemann.

———. 1984. "Direction and Misdirection in Peer Response." *College Composition and Communication 35* (October): 300–11.

Noddings, Nell. 1984. *Caring: A Feminine Approach to Ethics and Moral Education*. Berkeley: University of California Press.

North, Stephen. 1987. *The Making of Knowledge: Portrait of an Emerging Field*. Portsmouth, NH: Boynton Cook/Heinemann.

Orwell, George. [1936] 1988. "Shooting an Elephant." In *The Norton Reader: An Anthology of Expository Prose*, edited by Arthur Eastman et al., 768–74. 7th edition. New York: Norton.

Park, Robert Ezra. 1950. *Race and Culture*. Glencoe, IL: The Free Press.

Percy, Walker. 1975, 1984. "The Loss of the Creature." In *The Contemporary Essay*, edited by Donald Hall. New York: Bedford Books.

Perelman, Chaim, and L. Olbrechts-Tyteca. 1969. *The New Rhetoric: A Treatise on Argumentation*. Notre Dame, IN: University of Notre Dame Press.

Plato. [370 B.C.E.] 1990. *Phaedrus*. In *The Rhetorical Tradition: Readings Classical Times to the Present*, edited by Patricia Bizzell and Bruce Hertzberg. Boston: Bedford.

———. [375 B.C.E.] 1974. *The Republic*. Translated by Desmond Lee. London: Penguin Books.

Pratt, Mary Louise. 1991. "Arts of the Contact Zone." *Profession 91*: 33–40.

Princeton University. 1995. Application for admission.

Qualley, Donna. 1997. *Turns of Thought*. Portsmouth, NH: Boynton Cook/Heinemann.

Quinn, Laurie. 1996. "Cancer and the Cliché." Paper delivered at the Conference on Composition and Communication.

Rodriguez, Richard. 1994. "Late Victorians." In *The Art of the Personal Essay*, edited by Phillip Lopate, pp. 756–70. New York: Anchor Books.

———. 1982. *Hunger of Memory: The Education of Richard Rodriguez*. New York: Bantam.

Romano, Tom. 1995. *Writing with Passion: Life Stories, Multiple Genres.* Portsmouth, NH: Heinemann.

Rorty, Richard. 1979. *Philosophy and the Mirror of Nature.* Princeton, NJ: Princeton University Press.

Rose, Mike. 1989. *Lives on the Boundary.* New York: Penguin.

Rousseau, Jean-Jacques. [1767] n.d. *The Confessions of Jean-Jacques Rousseau.* New York: Modern Library.

Russo, Richard. 1986. *Mohawk.* New York: Vintage.

Schama, Simon. 1989. *Citizens: A Chronicle of the French Revolution.* New York: Knopf.

Shakespeare, William. [1623] 1988. *Hamlet.* New York: Bantam Books.

Shapiro, W. 1988. "Bush Scores Warm Win." *Time* (October 24): 18–20.

Simic, Charles. 1994. *The Unemployed Fortune Teller: Essays and Memoirs.* Ann Arbor: The University of Michigan Press.

Smiley, Jane. 1991. *A Thousand Acres.* New York: Fawcett Columbine.

Stafford, William. 1970, 1986. "A Way of Writing." In *To Compose: Teaching Writing in High School and College,* edited by Thomas Newkirk. Portsmouth: Heinemann.

Steele, Richard. [1710] 1994. "Twenty-four Hours in London." *The Art of the Personal Essay,* edited by Phillipe Lopate. New York: Anchor Books.

Steinem, Gloria. 1986. "Ruth's Song." In *Outrageous Acts and Everyday Rebellions.* New York: Signet.

Stevens, Wallace. 1973. *The Collected Poems of Wallace Stevens.* New York: Knopf.

Strickland, Ronald. 1990. "Confrontational Pedagogy and Traditional Literary Studies." *College English 52* (March): 291–300.

Thoreau, Henry David. [1854] 1983. *Walden and Civil Disobedience.* New York: Penguin.

Tobin, Lad. 1995a. "The Future of First-Year Writing Programs." Paper given at College Composition and Communication Conference, Milwaukee, Wisconsin.

———. 1995b. Introduction to *Taking Stock: The Writing Process Movement in the 90s.* Portsmouth, NH: Heinemann.

———. 1993. *Writing Relationships: What Really Happens in the Composition Class.* Portsmouth: Heinemann.

Twain, Mark [Samuel Clemens]. [1876] 1946. *The Adventures of Tom Sawyer.* New York: Grosset and Dunlap.

Wendell, Barrett. 1886, 1887. "Themes on Daily Life." Barrett Wendell Collection. Harvard University Archives.

———. 1891. *English Composition.* New York: Scribners and Sons.

White, E. B. 1977. "Once More to the Lake." In *Essays of E. B. White.* New York: Harper and Row.

Williams, William Carlos. 1968. "The Red Wheelbarrow." From *The Selected Poems of William Carlos Williams.* New York: New Directions.

Woolf, Virginia. [1942] 1994. "Street Hauntings." In *The Art of the Personal Essay,* edited by Phillip Lopate. New York: Anchor Books.

Index